Collins

# Cambridge IGCSE™

# English as a Second Language

## WORKBOOK

T0340505

Susan Anstey, Jane Gould, Mike Gould, Karen Harper,
Avril Kirkham, Julie Moore and Lorna Pepper

William Collins' dream of knowledge for all began with the publication of his first book in 1819.
A self-educated mill worker, he not only enriched millions of lives, but also founded a flourishing publishing house. Today, staying true to this spirit, Collins books are packed with inspiration, innovation and practical expertise.
They place you at the centre of a world of possibility and give you exactly what you need to explore it.

Collins. Freedom to teach.

Published by Collins
An imprint of HarperCollins*Publishers*
The News Building, 1 London Bridge Street, London, SE1 9GF, UK

HarperCollins*Publishers*
Macken House, 39/40 Mayor Street Upper, Dublin 1, D01 C9W8, Ireland

**Browse the complete Collins catalogue at www.collins.co.uk**

10 9 8 7 6 5 4

ISBN 978-0-00-849315-8

British Library Cataloguing-in-Publication Data
A catalogue record for this publication is available from the British Library.

Authors: Susan Anstey, Jane Gould, Mike Gould, Karen Harper, Avril Kirkham, Julie Moore and Lorna Pepper
Publisher: Elaine Higgleton
Product manager: Joanna Ramsay
Project manager/Series editor: Celia Wigley
Development editor: Lucy Cooper
Proofreader: Denise Cowle
Cover designer: Gordon MacGilp
Internal designer and illustrator: Life Lines Editorial Services and Ken Vail Graphic Design Ltd
Typesetter: Ken Vail Graphic Design Ltd
Production controller: Lyndsey Rogers

Printed in India by Multivista Global Pvt. Ltd.

This book contains FSC™ certified paper and other controlled sources to ensure responsible forest management.

For more information visit: www.harpercollins.co.uk/green

With thanks to everyone who has provided feedback and shared insights from their own teaching, examining and understanding of the students studying for this qualification: Abhinandan Bhattacharya (JBCN International School Oshiwara), Samar Sabat & Rula Kandalaft (Rosary Sisters High School), Suzanne Sheha (Nile Egyptian School), Christine Mariou (PASCAL Private English School), Vanessa Mitchell (Collège du Léman), Sioban Parker, Susan Anstey, Avril Kirkham, Karen Harper, and Fiona Leney.

The publishers gratefully acknowledge the permission granted to reproduce the copyright material in this book. Every effort has been made to trace copyright holders and to obtain their permission for the use of copyright material. The publishers will gladly receive any information enabling them to rectify any error or omission at the first opportunity.

The questions, example answers, marks awarded and/or comments that appear in this book were written by the authors. In examination, the way marks would be awarded to answers like these may be different.

Third-party websites and resources referred to in this publication have not been endorsed by Cambridge Assessment International Education.

# Introduction

The *Collins Cambridge IGCSE English as a Second Language Workbook* supports the Student's Book by offering further practice of English language skills to consolidate and develop your English language learning.

Intended to be used either in the classroom or at home, this write-in resource gives you additional opportunities to practise reading, writing, listening and speaking skills and to build your vocabulary. It can also be used as a stand-alone resource for self-study.

The Workbook provides learner support for the Cambridge IGCSE™ and IGCSE (9-1) English as a Second Language syllabuses (0510/0511/0991/0993) for examination from 2024. While the Student's Book provides full syllabus coverage, the Workbook offers additional opportunities to practise and consolidate the key language skills, leading to a deeper understanding of grammar and vocabulary. The clear explanations and practice activities are designed to help you apply the skills you're learning in the Student's Book and to improve your oral and written communication in English.

The Workbook is divided into six sections. Sections 1–5 focus on reading, writing, listening and speaking skills, covering key areas such as how to find and select information, how to write accurately, correct use of grammatical structures, writing for different purposes and how to approach listening tasks. The Speaking section gives invaluable advice on how to speak clearly and confidently, offering help with organising your ideas, pronunciation, how to express your opinions and how to develop a conversation.

Section 6 focuses on synonyms. Structured to follow the order of the topic-based chapters of the Student's Book, it highlights groups of similar words related to the topic, with useful definitions followed by practice exercises to help you increase your range of vocabulary and understand the subtle differences between words of similar meaning.

Both the Listening and Speaking sections include activities to help with listening comprehension, practical speaking and pronunciation. Audio files are provided to accompany some of the exercises – these are indicated on the page with an audio icon and a track number. The corresponding audio files can be found at www.collins.co.uk/internationalresources

Answer keys can be found at www.collins.co.uk/internationalresources.

We hope that this resource provides you with useful practice to deepen your learning and understanding of English.

# Contents

# Section 1: Reading skills and strategies

## ❶ Finding and selecting information

### SKIMMING AND SCANNING: UNDERSTANDING HEADINGS

**Subheadings** on websites or in information books and leaflets describe in a word or two the main information in that section.

Imagine you have found this website about teenage activity holidays in Spain. You want to find out more, so you click on 'Basketball camp' and see this menu of subheadings. By clicking on these, you would be able to find out more detail on that specific topic.

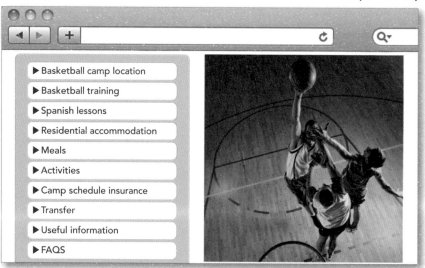

**1** Which heading will you click to find answers to the following questions?

**a)** Where is the camp based? Basketball camp location ...................................................

**b)** How can you improve your knowledge of Spanish? ...................................................

**c)** What sort of food will be provided? ...................................................

**d)** What are the sleeping arrangements like? ...................................................

**e)** Are there facilities for disabled people? ...................................................

### USING SKIMMING AND SCANNING TO FIND INFORMATION

Imagine you want to find out more detail about the activity holiday.

**2** **Skim read** the text on the next page and use the subheadings to decide which paragraph you will read to find the answers to these questions. Just write down the number of the subheading.

**f)** How many people will there be in a Spanish class? ...................................................

**g)** What kind of room will I stay in? ...................................................

**h)** When does the two-week course take place? ...................................................

**i)** What other activities are there besides basketball and Spanish lessons? ...................................................

**j)** What language is used for the basketball lessons? ...................................................

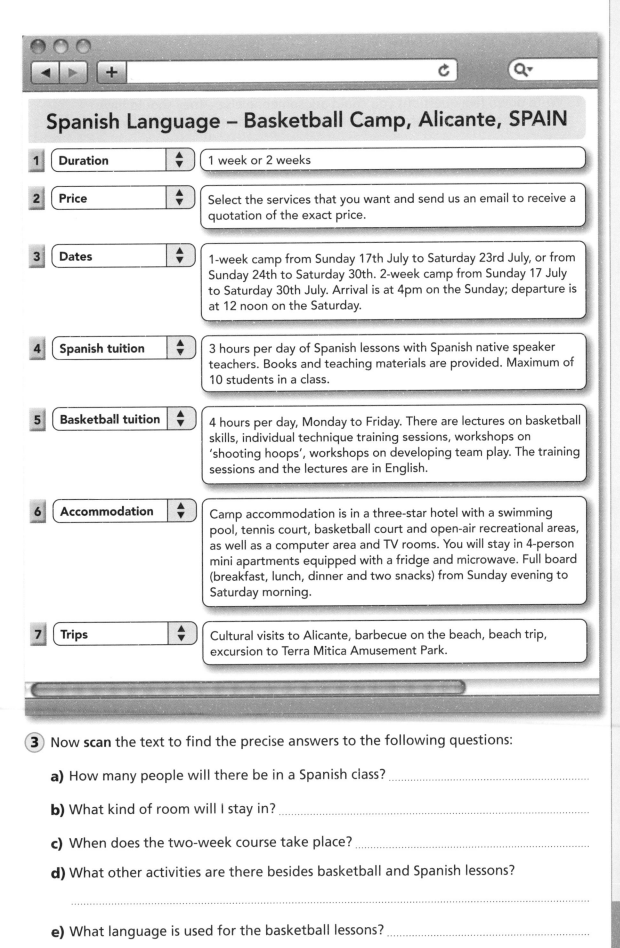

# Spanish Language – Basketball Camp, Alicante, SPAIN

**1** | **Duration** | 1 week or 2 weeks

**2** | **Price** | Select the services that you want and send us an email to receive a quotation of the exact price.

**3** | **Dates** | 1-week camp from Sunday 17th July to Saturday 23rd July, or from Sunday 24th to Saturday 30th. 2-week camp from Sunday 17 July to Saturday 30th July. Arrival is at 4pm on the Sunday; departure is at 12 noon on the Saturday.

**4** | **Spanish tuition** | 3 hours per day of Spanish lessons with Spanish native speaker teachers. Books and teaching materials are provided. Maximum of 10 students in a class.

**5** | **Basketball tuition** | 4 hours per day, Monday to Friday. There are lectures on basketball skills, individual technique training sessions, workshops on 'shooting hoops', workshops on developing team play. The training sessions and the lectures are in English.

**6** | **Accommodation** | Camp accommodation is in a three-star hotel with a swimming pool, tennis court, basketball court and open-air recreational areas, as well as a computer area and TV rooms. You will stay in 4-person mini apartments equipped with a fridge and microwave. Full board (breakfast, lunch, dinner and two snacks) from Sunday evening to Saturday morning.

**7** | **Trips** | Cultural visits to Alicante, barbecue on the beach, beach trip, excursion to Terra Mitica Amusement Park.

**3** Now **scan** the text to find the precise answers to the following questions:

**a)** How many people will there be in a Spanish class? .................................................

**b)** What kind of room will I stay in? .................................................

**c)** When does the two-week course take place? .................................................

**d)** What other activities are there besides basketball and Spanish lessons?

.................................................................................................................

**e)** What language is used for the basketball lessons? .................................................

## FINDING INFORMATION

Look again at the website on the previous page.

**1** Write down five questions you could ask someone else – they should have single-word or short phrase answers. Use the question prompts below.

What ........................................................................................................................ ?

When ....................................................................................................................... ?

How ......................................................................................................................... ?

Where will ............................................................................................................... ?

How many ............................................................................................................... ?

## GOING FURTHER

In reading and writing exercises, you often need to find specific information and details in a text. For example, look at this question and answers by two different students:

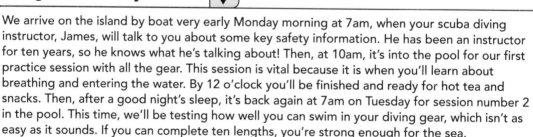

What kitchen equipment is provided for the holidaymakers?

**Adriana:** The four-person mini apartments are all equipped with a fridge and microwave.

**Karl:** A fridge and microwave.

Karl's answer gives the details that are required, but has no unnecessary information.

**2** Here are some details about a holiday schedule from another website. Read the text and then answer the three questions in single words or short phrases. Do not include any unnecessary information.

**Diving students – Days 1 and 2.** ⬍

We arrive on the island by boat very early Monday morning at 7am, when your scuba diving instructor, James, will talk to you about some key safety information. He has been an instructor for ten years, so he knows what he's talking about! Then, at 10am, it's into the pool for our first practice session with all the gear. This session is vital because it is when you'll learn about breathing and entering the water. By 12 o'clock you'll be finished and ready for hot tea and snacks. Then, after a good night's sleep, it's back again at 7am on Tuesday for session number 2 in the pool. This time, we'll be testing how well you can swim in your diving gear, which isn't as easy as it sounds. If you can complete ten lengths, you're strong enough for the sea.

**a)** What day and time do students arrive? ............................................................

**b)** Who will talk to the students? ........................................................................

**c)** Why is the first session vital? ........................................................................

**d)** What time will the session finish? ..................................................................

**e)** When will they begin session number 2? ........................................................

**f)** How will the instructors know if the students are strong enough swimmers for the sea? ..................................................................................................

## IDENTIFYING FACTS AND OPINIONS

**1** Which of these are **facts**, which are **opinions**? Circle the correct choice.

| | | |
|---|---|---|
| People use mobile phones too much. | *fact* | *opinion* |
| There are thirty students in our class. | *fact* | *opinion* |
| I received a text message at 5pm on Saturday. | *fact* | *opinion* |
| Speaking face to face is pointless; text messages are much more efficient. | *fact* | *opinion* |

## FACTS USED IN ARGUMENTS

**2** Facts can be used to make a point effectively or persuasively. Which *one* of these three facts would you choose if writing an article about how *good* mobile phones are? Tick your answer.

**Fact 1:** 60% of all people questioned thought mobile phones were a good thing. ☐

**Fact 2:** I questioned five friends. Three said they thought mobile phones were a good thing. ☐

**Fact 3:** 40% of people questioned were against mobile phones. ☐

> **GLOSSARY**
>
> **fact**      something you can prove beyond any reasonable doubt
>
> **opinion**    a personal point of view which others could disagree with

**3** Now write one sentence explaining your choice.

I chose Fact ............ because ................................................................................................................

## GOING FURTHER

**4** Read this short paragraph about mobile phones:

> It is absolutely clear that mobile phones are popular with just about everyone. You cannot argue with the facts, such as 60% of all people questioned being in favour of them. Ask anyone, and they will tell you all the wonderful things mobile phones can do. It is obviously true that they are an essential part of modern life.

How does the writer show the strength of his or her viewpoint here?

**a)** Underline any strong **adverbs** (words ending in *-ly* that give more emphasis, e.g. *totally*).

**b)** Circle **imperative verbs** (verbs that give commands or instructions, e.g. *Look … Take …*).

**5** Now write **two** sentences giving your own strong opinion about something. Choose from one of these topics, or one of your own:

- Cruelty to animals
- How much top sports or film stars are paid
- The way some people behave towards disabled people

Your first sentence should begin with a strong adverb. Your second should use an imperative verb – perhaps to do with what actions must be taken. Use this prompt if you wish:

It is totally/completely/utterly/absolutely ........................................ that ........................................

..........................................................................................................................................................

## GOING FURTHER

**Emotive words** are particularly powerful words that clearly show a writer's or speaker's attitude or strength of feeling.

The same situation can be written or spoken about in very different ways. Read this letter to a local newspaper:

I am writing to complain about what happened yesterday afternoon. A **mob** of noisy students shattered the peaceful atmosphere of our beautiful town yesterday afternoon. Their aim, they said, was to protest to the local council about the proposed closure of the town's library. Well, I thought they had a strange way of going about it. I saw twenty young men and women, screaming and waving their posters in the air, marching down our high street. They demanded to see the town mayor and hand over a **petition**. It is absolutely clear, in my view, that this disgraceful event should never have been allowed to take place. We must act immediately to prevent such a thing happening again. And get these **thugs** to face up to what they have done.

**Mrs I. M. Cross**

**GLOSSARY**

**mob** a large crowd intending to cause trouble

**petition** a written request signed by many people

**thugs** violent people

**6** Write down the facts of what happened. There should be no emotion in your facts. You could complete the sentences started below.

Yesterday, a group of ........................................................................................................

This took place in ........................................................................................................

The students wanted to ........................................................................................................

**7** Now decide which sentence in the letter directly describes what the writer's viewpoint of the protest march is. Write it here.

........................................................................................................

........................................................................................................

**8** Underline the key emotive words in the letter which show the writer's *opinion* of the students (e.g. *mob*).

**9** Select any further words or phrases that show the certainty of the writer's viewpoint and are used to make the argument more powerful. Write your choices below.

**a)** Find strong adverbs:

adverb 1: ........................................................................................................

adverb 2: ........................................................................................................

**b)** Find imperative verbs that express what should be done:

verb 1: ........................................................................................................

verb 2: ........................................................................................................

## EMOTIVE LANGUAGE

Words and phrases can be 'loaded' in negative or positive ways, as you have seen in the newspaper letter, for example, a *group/mob/gang*. Remember this when reading and also when writing to argue your own point of view.

**1** Look at the letter on the previous page again. Choose one word or phrase to sum up the writer's attitude to the students and their demonstration.

..........................................................................................................................................................

**2** Here are three headlines for a report about the march. Decide which:

- shows the students in the worst light (most negatively)
- shows them in the best light (most positively)
- is reasonably balanced (neutral).

Circle either negative, positive or neutral below.

STUDENT MOB SHATTER TOWN'S PEACE        *negative  positive  neutral*

LIBRARY'S SUPPORTERS MAKE POINT PEACEFULLY    *negative  positive  neutral*

STUDENTS MARCH IN PROTEST AGAINST LIBRARY CHANGE        *negative  positive  neutral*

**3** One of the students on the march read the letter. Here is her response. Circle the word in each case which presents her feelings *most strongly and accurately*.

I am writing to protest about the fantastic/dreadful/thoughtful letter sent in by Mrs Cross.

Our march through the town was violent/passionate/lively because we believe it is fairly/totally/a little bit wrong of the council to close our wonderful/dreadful/dull library.

For the writer to say we were 'screaming' is a complete exaggeration. We pleaded for/asked/demanded a meeting with the town mayor, but he would not listen.

## GOING FURTHER

You will have to argue your point of view on occasions.

**4** Now write a final paragraph for the student's letter, saying what you want to happen next. Make what you say sound emotive and strong. Try to:

- use the most powerful **nouns** (e.g. 'mob') or adjectives (e.g. 'passionate') you can think of
- include an **imperative verb** to show what should be done
- include powerful **adverbs** to go with adjectives (e.g. *'totally* clear', *'completely* true')

Write your paragraph here:

Finally, I would like to ................................................................................................................

..........................................................................................................................................................

..........................................................................................................................................................

..........................................................................................................................................................

## CLOSE READING FOR DETAIL

Read the following paragraphs from a magazine article about a special horse race in Mongolia, called the 'Mongol Derby', and then answer the questions below.

**Time yourself**: How long does it take you to do question 1? If you can complete it in under four minutes, you are doing well. Reread the text to check your answers and see how accurate you were.

# Riders prepare for Mongol Derby

## toughest horse race in the world

### The race

This summer, riders from around the world will have their first chance ever to tackle the Mongol Derby, a 1000-kilometre-long horse race through the harsh Mongolian landscape. It is being billed as the 'biggest, most dangerous equine affair on the planet'.

### The riders

Twelve of the 26 riders taking part are British, while other competitors come from Mongolia, Australia, South Africa and Spain. 'We had about 100 applications and selected just 26,' said a spokesman.

One British rider, Katy Willings, was attracted to the extreme physical challenge. 'To have the chance to experience one of the last truly **nomadic** cultures – riding across a true **wilderness** – made the whole thing irresistible,' she explained.

**GLOSSARY**

**nomadic**    describes people who travel from place to place with no permanent home

**wilderness**    a wild and difficult place to live in

**1** Answer the following questions:

**a)** How far do the riders have to travel during the course of the race?

................................................................................................................

**b)** How many riders are going to take part in the Mongol Derby?

................................................................................................................

**c)** Name **two** countries which will be represented by riders in the Mongol Derby.

.......................................................... and ..........................................

**d)** Which country does Katy Willings come from?

................................................................................................................

Now read this longer version of the text about the Mongolian horse race.
Then answer the next set of questions. Be accurate this time rather than fast.

# Riders prepare for Mongol Derby

## toughest horse race in the world

## The race

This summer, riders from around the world will have their first chance ever to tackle the Mongol Derby, a 1000-kilometre-long horse race through the harsh Mongolian landscape. It is being billed as the 'biggest, most dangerous equine affair on the planet'.

## The riders

Twelve of the 26 riders taking part are British, while other competitors come from Mongolia, Australia, South Africa and Spain. 'We had about 100 applications and selected just 26,' said a spokesman.

One British rider, Katy Willings, was attracted to the extreme physical challenge. 'To have the chance to experience one of the last truly nomadic cultures – riding across a true wilderness – made the whole thing irresistible,' she explained.

## How the race started

The idea of the race was thought up about four years ago. 'Because horses have a special importance in Mongolian culture, we decided to organise a horse race,' said an organiser. 'It is based on Genghis Khan's ancient postal system, where riders crossed Mongolia to Eastern Europe in about 14 days, changing horses every 40 kilometres along the way. It's a massive challenge.'

## What happens in the race

The race starts on 22 August at the ancient capital of the Mongol empire, Kharkhorin. The riders will change horses every 40 kilometres and more than 700 semi-wild Mongolian horses will be used during the race.

Each competitor is given a race map with the locations of each changing station, but they are essentially on their own. Throughout the race riders will stay with nomadic families, sleeping in tents, eating mutton and drinking the traditional fermented mares milk.

'The Mongol Derby is a real test of the rider's skill and endurance,' say the organisers. 'This will be no ordinary horse race – it's not just a test of the horse's speed.'

## How long it will last

The closing ceremony is planned for 5 September, but because this is the first race of its kind, organisers do not know how long riders will take. 'We're allowing two weeks for the slowest riders, but are expecting the fastest ones to complete in about five days – it just depends whether the riders are in for the race or for the cultural experience and adventure,' said the spokesman. 'And also, of course, they have paid quite a lot of money to take part.' The race costs $4450 to enter and competitors must raise a further $1600 for an organisation which supports rural communities in Mongolia.

(2) Answer the following questions in the spaces provided.

**a)** How many people applied to take part in the Mongol Derby?

..............................................................................................................................

**b)** Why did Katy Willings want to take part in the horse race? Give **two** reasons.

Reason 1:.................................................................................................................

..............................................................................................................................

..............................................................................................................................

Reason 2: ...............................................................................................................

..............................................................................................................................

**c)** How long did it take Genghis Khan's horse riders to carry a message right across the Mongolian Empire?

..............................................................................................................................

**d)** With whom will the riders spend the nights during the race?

..............................................................................................................................

**e)** What aspects of traditional Mongolian life will the riders experience?
Give **two** details.

..............................................................................................................................

..............................................................................................................................

**f)** What qualities does the Mongol Derby test in the competitors? Give **two** details.

..............................................................................................................................

..............................................................................................................................

The next two questions are slightly harder.

**g)** In what way is this horse race different from the usual kind of horse race?

..............................................................................................................................

..............................................................................................................................

**h)** Why might some riders not be in a great rush to finish the race, according to the organisers? Give **two** reasons.

Reason 1:.................................................................................................................

..............................................................................................................................

..............................................................................................................................

Reason 2:.................................................................................................................

..............................................................................................................................

..............................................................................................................................

## WRITING CONCISE ANSWERS

Here is the last paragraph again from the last text about the Mongol horse race.

### How long it will last

The closing ceremony is planned for 5 September, but because this is the first race of its kind, organisers do not know how long riders will take. 'We're allowing two weeks for the slowest riders, but are expecting the fastest ones to complete in about five days – it just depends whether the riders are in for the race or for the cultural experience and adventure,' said the spokesman. 'And also, of course, they have paid quite a lot of money to take part.' The race costs $4450 to enter and competitors must raise a further $1600 for an organisation which supports rural communities in Mongolia.

**1** Answer the questions below about this paragraph.

**a)** On which date will the prizes be given out?

.......................................................................................................................................

**b)** Although they cannot be sure, about how long do the organisers expect the race to last?

.......................................................................................................................................

**c)** What **three** reasons are suggested for the riders taking part in the race?

.......................................................................................................................................

.......................................................................................................................................

.......................................................................................................................................

 **TOP TIP** Remember, it's vital to read the question to see how many words you need to give as your answer.

Now look again at your answers above. Could they be shorter and still answer the question? Imagine you had given this answer for a):

**a)** At the closing ceremony on 5 September, although they can't be sure when the race will end.

Cross out the words which are not needed and leave those that still answer the question 'When?'.

## IDENTIFYING INTENTIONS

People's **intentions** (the ideas or plans of what they are going to do) can sometimes be hard to work out in texts. Look at this sentence:

> **If** I am given some money by my parents, **I might** go to Paris.

The use of 'if' and 'might' means: it is *not certain* the writer will get money, and it is also uncertain, then, whether he or she will go to Paris.

**1** Now look at: **When** I get some money from my parents, **I will** go to Paris. How is this different from the version above? Select and then circle the correct meaning:

**a)** It is *likely/quite likely/not likely at all* that he/she will be given money.

**b)** It is *likely/quite likely/not likely at all* that he/she will go to Paris.

> **TOP TIP**
>
> Looking closely at the forms of verbs, and the use of words such as *might, may, could, should* (known as modals) can help you understand the intentions and future actions of people in texts. These modals can make a big difference to meaning.

Here, a student, Pavel, talks about his love of horses and things he has already done, will definitely be doing in the future, or would like to do (if possible):

*Of course, when I go on holiday next year with my parents I'll be riding horses as we'll be staying at a large farm in Texas. I would love to take part in a long journey by horse across the mountains, but I can't do this until I've had more riding lessons. The farm owners won't let me go on a proper horse trek in the mountains unless they are sure I know what I am doing. I could take some riding lessons here in Poland before I leave.*

**2** Underline the modals and consider how they affect the meaning.

**3** Now, select and then circle *true* or *false* for each statement below. You will need to reread the text very carefully. The degree of certainty about what Pavel will do is shown by the modals used, such as *will, would, could*.

| | | |
|---|---|---|
| It is not very likely that Pavel is going to ride a horse on holiday. | true | false |
| Pavel is definitely going to ride a horse on holiday. | true | false |
| The place Pavel is going to stay at is a large farm. | true | false |
| Pavel is ready to go horse trekking. | true | false |
| It is impossible for Pavel to take riding lessons in his home country. | true | false |

# **2** Inferring and implying

## UNDERSTANDING WHAT IS IMPLIED BUT NOT ACTUALLY WRITTEN

Images can bring lots of ideas into your mind even when no other information is given.

**1** Find any **adjectives** in the word search below. For example, can you find 'alone'?

**2** Then, shade in or list those words which you think could be used to describe the woman in the photo.

**3** Finally, write here the two words you think best suit the picture:

Word 1: ........................................................................

Word 2: ........................................................................

| H | O | P | E | F | U | L | X |
|---|---|---|---|---|---|---|---|
| D | Z | X | L | T | N | T | C |
| N | B | A | A | J | W | J | O |
| H | A | P | P | Y | E | S | L |
| I | L | O | N | E | L | Y | D |
| B | O | R | E | D | L | Z | U |
| R | N | B | I | T | T | E | R |
| P | E | A | C | E | F | U | L |

When we **infer** something, we understand its meaning through the clues and details given. These suggest certain things, even if we are not told directly what is happening.

**4** What can you infer about the person from the image? Complete these sentences.

I think she is ........................................... because it appears that she is ...........................................

It could be that ........................................................... and ...........................................

## GOING FURTHER

(5) Now imagine that the photo on the previous page comes from an article in a newspaper. Here are three possible titles for the article. Under each one, make brief notes on what the article might be about. Then add a sentence saying why you think this.

# ALONE AND UNWANTED

The article could be about:

• How society ignores ......................................................................................................................................

• Friendship and ......................................................................................................................................

I think this because ......................................................................................................................................

# Memories Never Die

The article could be about:

......................................................................................................................................

......................................................................................................................................

I think this because ......................................................................................................................................

......................................................................................................................................

# PEACE AND QUIET AT LAST

The article could be about:

......................................................................................................................................

......................................................................................................................................

I think this because ......................................................................................................................................

......................................................................................................................................

## UNDERSTANDING TEXTS FROM CLUES

Here are the first few sentences of the article which goes with the photo of the woman.

## ALONE AND UNWANTED

A free bus pass from the government is welcome when you are 60, but it is not what Dora Edwards really wants. At 75, a widow with arthritis, living in a high-rise flat, and with no children or grandchildren, what she yearns for most is someone … anyone … to talk to. Surely that's not too much to ask? The government says it is listening, but it needs to do more than just listen. 'Who is looking after my real needs?' Dora wants to know.

**GLOSSARY**    **yearn**    want (something) very much

**1** You can work out the subject (the basic content of the article) by considering the clues. These are the words the writer has chosen – the vocabulary – and the factual information provided. Answer these questions about the article:

**a)** How old is Dora Edwards? .................................................................

**b)** What free item does the government give you if you reach the age of 60? ................

**c)** Where does Dora live? .................................................................

**d)** What does she suffer from? .................................................................

**e)** What do you find out about her family? (Find **three** things.)

1: .................................................................

2: .................................................................

3: .................................................................

**f)** What does she want more than a free bus pass, according to the article?

She would like .................................................................

## GOING FURTHER

**2** Now that you have understood the details of the extract, how would you describe the subject or main content of the article? You are not told directly: you have to work it out, to 'read between the lines' and infer.

Read carefully the five suggestions below. Then write A, B, C, D, E into the pyramid, putting the description that is closest to what the article is about at the TOP of the pyramid.

**A:** The things you can get for free when you are over the age of 60 in Britain.

**B:** The life of an older woman and what the government could do to make things better.

**C:** The importance of family.

**D:** Common illnesses suffered by elderly people.

**E:** Why high-rise flats are suitable for elderly people.

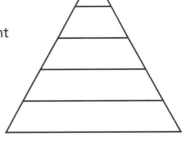

## INFERRING VIEWPOINT

What an article is *about* and the **viewpoint** of the writer are slightly different things. For example, even if we know what the article on the previous page is about, the writer does not mention his/her view. So, how can we tell what they think?

**(1)** Consider these choices made by the writer:

**a)** He/she uses the phrase *yearns for most* to describe Dora's needs. Is this a stronger or weaker phrase than: 'wants a bit' or 'would like'? Circle your answer below.

*stronger*      *weaker*

**b)** He/she uses a rhetorical question – one that does not expect an answer, or where the answer is obvious. Find this rhetorical question and write it below:

The rhetorical question used is ..................................................................................................................

**(2)** Here, a student has written about the article. Based on your reading of the article, circle the words you think best describe the writer's viewpoint.

> The writer is clearly <u>concerned about/happy with/bored of</u> the situation facing older people like Dora Edwards. He wants to make it clear that the government needs to <u>do more/do less/do nothing</u> to address the problem of loneliness for the old. <u>It is vital that/It would be nice if/It would be quite good if</u> they acted rather than simply listened.

Here is the next part of the article. It contains another person's views.

> But David Rimington, spokesperson for the local council of Dora Edward's town, takes a rather different view. 'We have offered Dora Edwards a regular visit from a social worker under a new scheme, "Call On Us", but I'm afraid she has not replied to our calls or letters. There is only so much we can do.'
>
> Dora admits that she is not keen to answer the phone after getting nuisance calls last year from young people in the flats below, and that she often throws away letters she thinks may be junk mail. However, even if this is true, surely someone could have called round, rather than just phoned or sent a letter?

**(3) a)** Now, consider the writer's viewpoint. What is David Rimington's view of the situation and how Dora has been treated? Tick the correct answer below:

**A:** The government has tried to do its best, but Dora has been difficult to contact. ☐

**B:** Dora is a nuisance and so the government should stop helping her. ☐

**C:** No one has helped Dora and he feels bad for her. ☐

**b)** Why has Dora not replied to the phone calls or letters offering her help? Give **two** reasons.

..................................................................................................................

..................................................................................................................

**(4)** Choose one word to describe Dora's attitude to receiving messages from the outside world. ..................................................................................................................

**(5)** Choose one word to describe David's attitude to Dora. Explain your choices.

..................................................................................................................

## USE OF CLEAR AND VIVID VOCABULARY

Some of the techniques used by writers of fictional stories are also used in articles, letters and essays. For example, the **use of clear and vivid vocabulary** to create a picture in the reader's mind.

Read this extract from someone remembering a childhood experience:

> One of my earliest memories as a child was walking through a dark forest on my own. The giant trees seemed to come alive and surround me. A narrow path snaked through the trees and disappeared into the darkness. I remember running away as fast as I could, trying to escape my own imagination. I promised myself never to read stories about old legends again, and never to listen to Uncle's scary tales around the fire. But all of this was too late. At that age, it wouldn't have mattered what I had read or seen or heard. The giant trees coming alive were my own creation. If, indeed, they had come to life, I'm sure they would have been less awful in reality than in my vivid imagination where they were created.
>
> Years later, in my thirties, after having lived away for a long time, I revisited my village. I did that same walk through the forest. The path seemed straighter, the trees smaller, stubby and insignificant. What could have possibly made me feel so afraid back then?

**1** Circle the words below that best describe the writer's state of mind as a girl.

*relaxed    worried    anxious    terrified    confident    sad    angry    confused*

**2** What else can you work out about the girl's feelings from the vocabulary she uses?

**a)** When she says *the giant trees seemed to come alive and surround me,* what does she mean?

She means that the movement and shapes of the trees looked like living creatures in her mind

and ............................................................................................................................

**b)** What does *A narrow path snaked* suggest about the path and how it looked?

It was ............................................................................................................................

**c)** When the writer says *I remember running away as fast as I could from my own imagination,* what does this mean?

It means she was running away from ..................................................................................

**d)** How does the use of vocabulary in the last paragraph suggest the writer was older?

It is less emotional and ...................................................................................................

## GOING FURTHER

**3** The last paragraph suggests that the writer changed as she got older. Find two things that appear to have changed about the forest.

..........................................................................................................................................

..........................................................................................................................................

# ③ Using information

### MULTIPLE MATCHING QUESTIONS

The following text is an article about how four young people spend their holidays.

## GOING ON HOLIDAY

### A George

Every year, George spends the whole month of August in the South of France. He always goes away with his parents and two brothers. The family take their boat with them and camp near to the beach. The whole family enjoy swimming, sunbathing and water sports. George and his two brothers' favourite activity is water skiing and they compete with each other to see who can be the best! The evenings are spent dining out at various restaurants and, as George and his family come from a cold country, they love the warm evenings and eating outdoors. George is fluent in French, so he has asked his parents whether they could have a change next year and visit North Africa, preferably still on the coast.

### B Yusuf

Yusuf lives in a country where there is a lot of desert. So, in the summer, the whole family prefer to be in a cooler climate and visit different capital cities in Europe. Yusuf speaks English, but he also likes to try speaking other languages, so he always takes a phrase book and dictionary with him in order to communicate with people in their own language. However, last year, the family decided to do something different and have a winter holiday in America. Yusuf found that he had a natural ability for skiing and snowboarding, and was soon spending all day in the mountains. Next summer, Yusuf's family are planning a trip to Budapest, but have agreed that Yusuf can go skiing in the winter with his friends instead.

### C Louise

Louise lives in an apartment in the city centre, on the 14th floor. She loves the view from her bedroom and the hustle and bustle of living in a large city. Nevertheless, at the weekend Louise's family escape to their house in the country overlooking a lake. The house is just a few hours' drive from the city. Every summer they meet up with all the uncles, aunties and cousins for a month's holiday together in the house. She has many happy memories of sailing on the lake, but leaves the water skiing to her cousins! Louise has never been abroad, so she has been asking her parents to have a change next year and go to another country. She hopes it will be an English-speaking country so she can try communicating in another language.

### D Alice

Alice and her family live in the mountains and she has been skiing and snowboarding for as long as she can remember. In fact, when there was a lot of snow in winter, Alice sometimes had to ski to school! In the summer, however, the family enjoy travelling to more exotic countries and never go back to the same place. Luckily for Alice her parents speak several languages, as she is always too nervous to try even a few words! Last year, they went on safari in Africa. Alice was pleasantly surprised with the weather as she thought it would be really hot. Alice wanted to camp, but the rest of the family were too nervous so they stayed in a safari lodge. The highlight of the holiday was when she saw a whole family of elephants bathing in a lake. Having already visited Australia and America, Alice is hoping her parents will choose the Far East next year so that she can see more elephants!

The questions below are about the people (A–D) described in each paragraph.

For each question write the correct letter A, B, C or D

Which person

**a)** lives in a hot country .........

**b)** loves water skiing .........

**c)** goes on holiday in their own country .........

**d)** camps with their family .........

**e)** enjoys winter sports holidays .........

**f)** spends holidays with the extended family .........

**g)** goes somewhere different every year .........

**h)** prefers holidays by the sea .........

**i)** doesn't like speaking another language .........

**j)** will not be going away with their family next year .........

## GOING FURTHER

Write four more questions on the text, or write a similar paragraph about yourself.

## HANDWRITING

Good handwriting is important for clear written communication. All your letters should be clearly formed. Capital letters should all be bigger than lower case letters.

**(1)** Copy these sentences in your normal handwriting.
The quick brown fox jumps over the lazy dog.

......................................................................................................................................................................

Jim just quit and packed extra bags for Liz Owen.

......................................................................................................................................................................

William Jex quickly caught five dozen Republicans.

......................................................................................................................................................................

A large fawn jumped quickly over white zinc boxes.

......................................................................................................................................................................

Five or six big jet planes zoomed quickly by the tower.

......................................................................................................................................................................

These sentences are all called *pangrams*. You do not need to know this word, but can you guess what pangrams are?

**(2)** Here are two handwritten responses to the same task. Go through each and circle any handwriting that is unclear or difficult to read and any grammatical mistakes such as missing or incorrect capital letters.

> I have just started this wonderful job in Freetown. I am working in an Eco-Friendly cafe making fruit smoothies for tourists; Yesterday a party of 20 Russian school-girls rushed in and we were so busy!

> i have just started this wonderful new job in freetown. I am working in an eco-friendly cafe making Fruit smoothies and tropical juices for Tourists. I love meeting new people; Yesterday a party of 20 Russian school-girls rushd in and wewere So busy!

## MAKING NOTES UNDER HEADINGS

Read this article from a local newspaper. Afterwards, you are going to produce three lists of details under given headings.

**(1)** Before you write anything:
- Skim read the article to get a general sense of how the information is organised.
- Read the three headings in question 2 (below) very carefully.
- Read the article more carefully. Take three different coloured pencils and underline the details relating to each heading in a different colour.
- Then write your lists – your notes – under the correct headings.
- Remember that notes should not be full sentences.

# 'Be a friend' to your community

Have you ever thought what it is like to be alone, elderly and with no one to care for you? Unfortunately, there are many older people just like this in the town. So, I'm asking you, our readers, as the editor of this paper, to help make things better. This will be our newspaper's **campaign** this year.

Why are we doing it? It all started when we heard that the council had sent leaflets to everyone in the town explaining that they would have to spend 20% more on employing carers to visit old people living alone. They said that people were just not doing enough to make sure that older neighbours and residents were looked after. The money for this care would mean that other services, such as recycling, would need to be cut.

It's not just the fact that not enough people are visiting older people or relatives to check that they are okay. As a newspaper, we had noticed for ourselves how the town is not very suitable for older people to visit. There are no benches to rest on in the main shopping street. The nearest public toilets are up a steep hill, and the only lift in the main library is broken.

In addition, the bus shelter is covered in graffiti and the timetable is in tiny print that no one, however young or old, could read.

So our paper wants to do something to improve matters. Join us and help. We intend to do two things. Firstly, we need volunteers to join our scheme to visit older people who can't get out of the house and would like some company just for a chat, or to do a few basic jobs. Secondly, we need young, fit and active readers to help us make the town more welcoming for older people. With the agreement of the council we have arranged for as many of our readers as are interested to help clean up the bus shelter, install benches and improve signs. To make sure everyone is involved, those who do not want to spend time cleaning or improving the town centre could make their first visit to some of the older people the council has told us about.

Please come and help. The more of us there are, the quicker we can get the jobs done, and the more people can be visited. Meet us outside the Market Coffee Shop at 10am. If you have any queries, you can contact me, the editor, Miles Smith, here at the newspaper, or my assistant editor, Orla Martinez.

| GLOSSARY | **campaign** action organised to get something done |

**2** Make your notes under each heading.

Who readers should contact if they are interested in helping

- .........................................................................................................................................................
- .........................................................................................................................................................

The problems the 'Be a friend' campaign has seen in the town

- .........................................................................................................................................................
- .........................................................................................................................................................
- .........................................................................................................................................................
- .........................................................................................................................................................
- .........................................................................................................................................................

Actions that the campaign will carry out this weekend

- .........................................................................................................................................................
- .........................................................................................................................................................
- .........................................................................................................................................................
- .........................................................................................................................................................
- .........................................................................................................................................................

## GOING FURTHER

**3** Make notes below of details which show that the organisers are concerned for the health and happiness of the elderly people

- .........................................................................................................................................................
- .........................................................................................................................................................
- .........................................................................................................................................................
- .........................................................................................................................................................

# ORGANISING INFORMATION, CREATING HEADINGS

Texts are often split into sections, with each section about a slightly different thing.

**1** Here is a paragraph from an article about 'storm chasing'. Read it carefully.

A person who chases storms is, not surprisingly, known as a 'storm chaser', or even just a 'chaser', but their reasons for chasing storms vary. For many, their main intention is to witness a **tornado** at first hand, so actually getting up close to them and experiencing the fear and excitement is their key objective. However, others chase thunderstorms and get great pleasure simply because they enjoy seeing unusual or beautiful cloud structures and **skyscapes**, or want to watch a **barrage** of hail and lightning.

**GLOSSARY**

**tornado**    a violent wind storm consisting of a tall column of air which spins round very fast and causes a lot of damage

**skyscape**    (here) a wide view of the sky

**barrage**    a large number of attacks directed at someone or something

**2** Which of the following headings best describes what this paragraph is about? Tick the best answer below. Be careful – do not find just one small thing in the heading that matches the paragraph. The best summary headings will cover the *overall* focus of the paragraph.

**A:** The dangers of storm chasing ☐

**B:** Why some people chase storms ☐

**C:** How lovely storms can be ☐

> **TOP TIP**
>
> **Information** and **explanation texts** tend to describe how and why things happen or people act as they do, so it is likely your headings and notes will do this too.

**3** Read the paragraph again. Write down **three** reasons why people chase storms.

**A:** ...............................................................................

**B:** ...............................................................................

**C:** ...............................................................................

Now read the remainder of the article about storm chasing.

Storm chasers are not often paid for what they do, but it would be fair to say that they often provide valuable on-the-ground help for weather agencies and local government in the USA when storms are approaching. They upload photos or data from the equipment they carry with them, and this can help agencies predict the path of storms or confirm whether their own observations are correct or not. On the other hand, providing dramatic photos or videos of storms and tornadoes from the very spot where they are happening can earn them good money if television or news networks are willing to pay. Or they can be sold to picture agencies.

Storm chasing has probably been around for many years. Most people remember their first storm as a child and the excitement and fear it brought, and for some it becomes a career. Perhaps the first real storm chaser was a man called David Hoadley (1938– ), who first chased North Dakota storms in 1956; he used data from local area weather offices and was the founder of *Storm Track* magazine. Another man, Neil B Ward (1914–1972) worked with the Oklahoma Highway Patrol to study storms and made it possible for larger organisations to chase storms using detailed research.

Increasingly, storm chasing has entered popular culture, with perhaps the key event being the release and success of the film *Twister* in 1996. It was the second most successful film, financially, of 1996 in the USA (the first being the box-office smash, *Independence Day*, which was not about storm chasing, of course), suggesting a really strong interest in the subject. However, 'real' storm chasers complained that it gave an inaccurate and over-simplified view of the subject. This did not reduce the public's enthusiasm, however, and the 2007–2011 series, 'Storm Chasers' on the Discovery Channel actually led to more people taking it up.

Nowadays, storm chasing is an increasingly sophisticated activity with participants learning about meteorology to help their quest and using satellite-based tracking systems to pursue or predict the paths of storms. Digital video, digital SLR cameras and GPS phones have all made communication of data and images easier and quicker, but there are still many storm chasers who trust instinct and their own senses to be in the right – or wrong – place!

## MAKING FURTHER NOTES

The first paragraph of the article continues the theme of 'why storm chasers chase storms', but it deals with two categories of storm chasers: those who do it for money and those who do not.

**4** Make brief notes under these two headings:

Those who do not chase storms for money – how they are helpful

- .................................................................................................................................
- .................................................................................................................................

Those who chase storms to make money – how they make money

- .................................................................................................................................
- .................................................................................................................................

**5** The first paragraph is mostly written in the **present tense** (*They upload photos* …).

**a)** What verb tense is mostly used in the second paragraph?

.................................................................................................................................

Give one example:

.................................................................................................................................

**b)** Are we told mostly about people, processes or specific events?

.................................................................................................................................

**c)** What heading or title would you give to your set of notes for this paragraph as a result?

My title would be: .................................................................................................................

**6** Now select three key points made in paragraph 2 about memories of storms and/or important storm chasers.

Point 1: ...........................................................................................................................

Point 2: ...........................................................................................................................

Point 3: ...........................................................................................................................

**(7)** Finally, reread the last two paragraphs.

Here, a student has chosen a heading and key points for Paragraph 3.

Paragraph 3 heading: US box-office smashes, 1996

Point 1: storm chasing has entered popular culture with perhaps the key event being the release and success of the film 'Twister' in 1996.

Point 2: 'Independence Day' was a box-office smash

Point 3: the TV series, 'Twister' led to more storm chasing by the public

**a)** What is wrong with these notes? Is the heading accurate?

It is a good/bad heading because .......................................................................................................................

**b)** Is point 1 in note form? How could it be expressed more simply? Write a better version here:

Point 1: success of 'Twister' was .......................................................................................................................

**c)** Is point 2 relevant or irrelevant?

It is relevant/irrelevant because the film 'Independence Day' is ..............................................................

**d)** Which part of point 3 is correct and which is incorrect? Cross out the wrong information and then write the correct information in its place:

The TV series 'Twister' led to more storm chasing by the public.

Now write the correct version:

The .......................................................................................................................

**(8)** Now write your own heading and notes for Paragraph 4 in the spaces below.

Paragraph 4 heading: .......................................................................................................................

Point 1: .......................................................................................................................

Point 2: .......................................................................................................................

Point 3: .......................................................................................................................

> **TOP TIP** Do not rewrite in full the points or sentences from the text. Leave out unnecessary words. For example, in the third paragraph, you would not need to include all the definite articles, and could put: success of film, Twister, 1996 – no need for *the*, *in* and *so on*.

# Section 2: Writing for accuracy

## ① Sentences

### WHAT IS A SENTENCE?

Punctuation marks help us understand the meaning of a sentence. They can end with a full stop, question mark or exclamation mark.

| | |
|---|---|
| Make a **statement**: | The crowd roared enthusiastically. |
| Ask a **question** or make a request: | How does this machine work?<br>Do you honestly expect us to believe that? |
| Give a **command** or **instruction**: | Turn right by the mosque. |
| **Exclaim**, to stress a point or show strength of feeling: | How awful that hat is!<br>What a pity! |

**①** What sort of sentences are shown in a) to d) below? Write on the line the type of sentence shown. The first one has been done for you.

**②** Then, for each question, tick what type of text it might have come from.

**a)** *The music festival took place at the outdoor arena.* statement .....................................

*The line-up was great, with some of my favourite bands*

*and singers performing.* statement .....................................

*Rihanna was fantastic!* exclamation .....................................

**What type of text?**
email to a head teacher ☐     letter ☑     dictionary entry ☐

**b)** *What was that noise?* .....................................

*He stopped for a moment and put his backpack*

*down. Surely all the tigers had died out years ago?* .....................................

*Then he heard a growl and the sound of something*

*crashing through the undergrowth. It was a tiger.* .....................................

**What type of text?**
email to a friend ☐     adventure story ☐     diary ☐

**c)** *Feed Timmo each morning.* .....................................

*Put the bins out for collection on Thursdays.* .....................................

*Water the plants on the patio. Please don't forget to post that cheque!* .....................................

**What type of text?**
mystery story ☐     newspaper report ☐     list left by parents while on holiday ☐

**d)** *What a day!* .....................................

*I met my favourite pop star and got his autograph.* .....................................

*How cool is that?* .....................................

**What type of text?**
diary entry ☐     information text ☐     newspaper report ☐

# TYPES OF SENTENCE

## SIMPLE SENTENCES

A **simple sentence** is usually short and contains a **subject** (the person or thing who does the action of the verb) and a **verb** (a doing or being word), and can be useful for clear explanations and instructions. For example:

*I* [subject] *sat* [verb] *at the station.*

**1** Add a **verb** to these simple sentences:

**a)** The atmosphere was amazing. She ................................................ to the front row.

**b)** The crowd ................................................

**c)** Then, it all went quiet. The music ................................................

## COMPOUND SENTENCES

A **compound sentence** can be used to balance ideas or join two short or simple sentences of equal importance. You can use 'and', 'or' and 'but' to join the two sentences. For example:

*Our team played well **and** the players showed all their skills.*

**2** Now write compound sentences about a meal you had recently.

**a)** The ................................................ was tasty and the ................................................

**b)** My ................................................ did the cooking, but ................................................ did the ................................................

**c)** However, I prefer going out to eat.

**d)** I am happy to go to ................................................ or I like ................................................

## GOING FURTHER

Short sentences can be used in creative ways, too. Here, the short sentences suggest time is passing slowly (s = subject; v = verb).

s  v                          s        v        s        v
*I* **sat** *at the station.* *The clock* **ticked**. *He* **wasn't coming**.

**3** Create three or four short simple sentences from this long sentence to make it seem tense or full of drama. You can add exclamation marks or question marks if you wish.

*I waited by the door for my exam results to come and watched as people went past my window until I finally heard steps up the garden path.*

Start with: I waited by the door. Would my exam results ever ................................................

................................................

**4** Now write three or four short simple sentences to create tension when describing an exam or test situation. Start with:

Marcia sat in the exam hall. The ................................................

................................................

## COMPLEX SENTENCES

A longer **complex sentence** can add further information, provide contrast, show cause and effect, and so on. It can be made up of lots of parts built around a main idea.

Let's take the exam room situation …

main part of sentence
**You could hear a pin drop**

extra 'bit' of information
*although the room was full of students.*

Usually the extra 'bit' does not make sense on its own or sounds unfinished.

**5** Draw lines to match the main and supporting parts of these sentences.

*Although it was raining,*

*Even though we queued for five hours,*

*Because we were forced to wait,*

*we couldn't get any tickets.*

*we missed the last train home.*

*we managed to keep dry.*

**6** Now complete the following sentences, adding further information. You can base your ideas on a wasted trip to see a match and the journey home.

**a)** I arrived home ........................................... although I managed to get a taxi.

**b)** My older brother said that ........................................... even though he was sympathetic.

**c)** My mum kindly ........................................... because I was so fed up.

In d) below, the main part and the extra part have been swapped around for variety. Complete it in the same way.

**d)** While I realise that I should not have gone without tickets, I am determined to ...........................................
...........................................

**7** In the following paragraphs:
- underline the compound sentence
- circle the complex sentence
- highlight the simple sentence(s).

**a)** *The market street was incredibly dark and there were suspicious figures barely visible in the shadows. They seemed to be watching. Even though we were travelling light, we were dripping with sweat.*

**b)** *A neon light flashed on and off. Because it was so late, all the hotels were shut. We walked up and down and we phoned all the hotel numbers. It was no good. Everything was closed.*

**c)** *Even though we were beginning to get worried, Alicia remained cool. She led us to the beach. There were lots of young people partying and there was plenty of space for us to sit. It was almost morning.*

## DEVELOPING SENTENCES WITH PHRASES

First of all, check your understanding of **nouns** (the names we give to things, people and ideas).

> Nouns can also be categorised as:
> - Common: *cat, dog, man, woman, dinner*
> - Proper: *Nairobi, Gandhi, Victorians, Ramadan, The Lord of the Rings*
> - Collective: *a **herd** of cattle, a **crowd** of people, a **team** of footballers*
> - Abstract: *hope, fear, loneliness, fatherhood*

 **TOP TIP** If some of the following are true of a word, it is likely to be a noun:
- it may follow the words/phrases a, the, a few, some
- it changes form to show singular, plural or possession, for example: girl, girls, girl's, girls'

**1** Find the nouns in this pile of words and then sort them under the four headings in the table below: common, proper, collective and abstract.

book   flock   lemonade   tasty   better   curiously   Cape Town   believable   tablecloth
motherhood   engine   love   lunch   dull   gang   audience   boredom   tribe
cup   under   belief   Koreans   suspicion   Sydney   Walt Disney   lovely   bored   Paris

| Common | Proper | Collective | Abstract |
|--------|--------|-----------|----------|
|        |        |           |          |
|        |        |           |          |
|        |        |           |          |
|        |        |           |          |
|        |        |           |          |
|        |        |           |          |

**Noun phrases** are very important in writing because they allow you to pack a lot of information into a few words. The noun phrase has a noun as the **head word** (the part around which everything else grows). For example, in the following sentence the head word is the noun *soup*:

> *Enjoy my tasty, homemade soup, packed with the goodness of home-grown vegetables.*

The soup is *tasty*; it is *homemade*; it is *packed with the goodness of home-grown vegetables*.

Sentences such as this can contain more than one noun phrase. For example:

> *A nasty-looking, striped, buzzing insect* from *my overgrown garden* landed on *my pale and exposed leg*.

**2** Try building up the following sentences by adding noun phrases to them. Add **adjectives** and/or **nouns** in the spaces provided.

**a)** A beautiful, .............................. butterfly from the .............................. field near my house landed on our ..............................

**b)** That .............................. film we went to see was the best I have seen all year!

## USING PAIRS OF WORDS OR PHRASES

You can also help readers understand your writing by using pairs of words to join sentences, for example, *either … or*:

● *You could go home to collect the shirt. You could ask your brother to bring the shirt here.*

● **Either** *go home to collect the shirt* **or** *ask your brother to bring it here.*

These joining words are called **connectives**.

**1** Join the following pairs of simple sentences using the pairs of connectives in the box below. You may need to change punctuation and the order of words.

> *Not only … but also …    Although … nevertheless …*
>
> *If … then …          Either … or*

**a)** You want to go. I will come with you.

.............................................................................................................................

**b)** We could have pizza at the Italian restaurant. We could have curry at home.

.............................................................................................................................

**c)** He is not very good at sports. He always does his very best at sports.

.............................................................................................................................

**d)** My friend enjoys playing volleyball. He enjoys taking part in competitions.

.............................................................................................................................

> **TOP TIP**
>
> Watch your use of commas! Try not to separate parts of a sentence with a comma when you need a connective or a new sentence. For example:
> * *We went to the show, I didn't enjoy it.* should be …
> * *We went to the show but I didn't enjoy it.*

## GOING FURTHER

To develop your writing to a higher level, you need to learn to use a range of sentence types and lengths.

**2** Take one of the sentences you made in task 1 and develop it into a paragraph. Write at least one simple sentence, one compound sentence and one complex sentence following the guidance on these pages. Use the same topic to link them together into one paragraph.

# MORE WAYS OF JOINING SENTENCES

## USING WORDS ENDING IN -ING

Another way to join sentences is to use words ending in -ing. These are called **present participles**, for example, *singing*. They come from verbs but act like adjectives. Look at these examples.

> <u>Singing</u>, the girl walked along the road. (Singing describes 'the girl'.)

> <u>Giggling</u>, the two friends made their way home.

Present participles can be joined with other words into phrases. For example, *singing a terrible love song*, or *giggling helplessly*. These phrases can be used in sentences:

> Singing a terrible love song, the girl walked along the road.

> Giggling helplessly, the two friends made their way home.

We can use these **participles** or **participle phrases** to join ideas together. So,

> The man was eating a biscuit. The man made a phone call.

can be joined together and written as:

> Eating a biscuit, the man made a phone call.

> **TOP TIP** Note how, when the phrase is at the start of a sentence like this one, it is separated from the rest of it by a comma.

**(1)** Now use a participle or a participle phrase to join these pairs of sentences:

**a)** The dog growled. The dog gnawed its bone.

*Growling, the dog gnawed its bone.* ...........................................................

**b)** Hussain ran away from the fierce dog. Hussain tripped over a rock.

..............................................................................................................

**c)** Frederich enjoyed every minute. Frederich danced along with the music.

..............................................................................................................

**d)** Marina opened the window and looked out. Marina shouted out to her friends.

..............................................................................................................

**e)** The snake hissed. The snake slid in through the window.

..............................................................................................................

**f)** The runner slowed down. The runner panted heavily.

..............................................................................................................

**g)** Scott put his pen down and sighed. Scott left the exam room.

..............................................................................................................

## GOING FURTHER

Here is an example of a slightly different participle phrase.

*The water drained slowly from the swimming pool choked with old leaves.*

This uses the **past participle** which ends in *-ed*, again to act more like an adjective. In this case, *choked with old leaves* describes the noun *swimming pool*.

Not only do participle phrases allow you to add information to your ideas, they also mean you can begin sentences in a variety of ways.

**2** Can you add your own present or past participle phrases to these sentences?

**a)** The shopkeeper, ........................................................ at the counter, watched the woman carefully. (suggested verb: *stand*)

**b)** ........................................................ the Cup was our first victory ever. (suggested verb: *win*)

**c)** ........................................................ they soon cleared up after the floods. (suggested verb: *help*)

**d)** ........................................................ she is popular all over the world. (suggested verbs: *love, admire*)

**e)** ........................................................, I thanked everyone at the party. (suggested verb: *to be pleased*)

Using participle and noun phrases to build longer sentences and add detail is a really useful skill for making your writing clearer and more informative.

**3** Describe your visit to a new shopping centre. Below is a basic outline of the writing. You can change and add to it using the skills you have learnt. Try to add something about:
- your excitement at seeing the centre for the first time
- which shops you visited – add details about one in particular
- what you thought about the shopping centre as a whole.

Remember to use a range of different sentence structures, and include some participle phrases and noun phrases.

I went to the new shopping centre yesterday. It was in the middle of town and ........................

........................................................................................................................................

I couldn't decide which one to go into. Then I chose one and looked round it. It had ........................

........................................................................................................................................

I thought they looked ........................................................................................................

........................................................................................................................................

Afterwards, I went ........................................................................................................

........................................................................................................ I left at 7pm.

## JOINING IDEAS TO MAKE MORE INTERESTING SENTENCES

Imagine you have these notes for a summary about Europe.

> ● London – capital city of England – population of over 9 million

You could write a compound sentence:

> *London is the capital of England and it has a population of over 9 million.*

To make it more interesting, you could add variety to your sentence structures, for example, by using the word 'which':

> *London, which is the capital city of England, has a population of over 9 million.*

Or by using brackets:

> *London (the capital of England) has a population of over 9 million.*

**1** Now use the following notes to write a paragraph about one of the other capital cities of Europe. Choose a variety of sentence structures. Check that you have used punctuation correctly.

> ● Paris – capital city of France – population: 2.2 million people – River Seine flows through Paris
> ● Vienna – capital city of Austria – population: 1.9 million people – River Wien flows through Vienna

Your paragraph:

........................................................................................................................

........................................................................................................................

........................................................................................................................

........................................................................................................................

## GOING FURTHER

You could begin your paragraph about Paris by comparing it with London (in terms of size):

> **Smaller than** London, Paris ...........................................................................

**2** Try rewriting your paragraph from task 1 using comparatives.

Your new paragraph:

........................................................................................................................

........................................................................................................................

........................................................................................................................

........................................................................................................................

## USING THE ACTIVE AND THE PASSIVE

**Active** and **passive** verb forms allow you to change the tone and effect of your sentences. They also add variety to your sentence structures.

**Active:** *I noticed the fire in the shop and I called the police.*

*The subject of the sentence is present and 'does' the action (noticing the fire/calling the police)*

**Passive:** *The fire was noticed and the police were called.*

*The subject (the person who noticed the fire) is missing from the sentence, so the text seems more objective and 'distant'.*

The passive style is especially useful for formal accounts which need a sense of authority, and where facts are more important than emotions.

**1** Underline the use of any passive verb forms in the following text.

*The shark was observed at 7am breaking the surface of the water approximately half a mile from the shore. Local coastguards were alerted and the shark was guided out to sea to safer areas before any harm was done to tourists.*

**2** **a)** Which of these forms of text do you think the text is most likely to come from?

**A:** teenager's diary ☐

**B:** encyclopedia entry about sharks ☐

**C:** news report ☐

**D:** police report ☐

**b)** In one sentence, explain why it would fit the form of text you have chosen:

I think this style fits ................................................ because ........................................................

........................................................................................................................................................

**3** Finally, read this second version of the text written in the **active voice**.

*I thought 'wow' when I saw the shark at around seven this morning in the sea, I guess about half a mile or so out. Tourists were swimming right near it! So I called the coastguards and they acted so quickly and guided it out to sea before it could do any damage.*

**a)** Underline the active verb forms in the text above.

**b)** Which of these forms of text do you think this text comes from?

**A:** eye-witness interview ☐

**B:** police report ☐

**C:** poem ☐

**D:** encyclopedia entry about sharks ☐

## ② Paragraphs

### WHAT IS A PARAGRAPH?

A **paragraph** is a group of sentences, usually about a single topic – the same main idea, theme, person or event.

Read this example:

> *Our school swimming pool needs repairing. There is no diving board, the tiles around the outside are covered in weeds and are broken, and there is a leak which means the water drains away quickly. The leak is probably at the deep end as you can always see muddy bubbles coming to the surface.*

**(1)** What is this paragraph mainly about (what topic links all the points made)?

**A:** the missing diving board ☐

**B:** the leak ☐

**C:** the poor state of the swimming pool as a whole ☐

**D:** the tiles ☐

**Topic sentences** can help you structure paragraphs by acting as an introduction. For example:

> *Our school swimming pool needs repairing* – you then go on to say what the problems are.
>
> *There are three jobs that need to be done to repair the pool* – which you then name.

These in turn can help structure your whole essay.

**(2)** A building company has sent an email to the school's head teacher about repairing the swimming pool. Unfortunately, some of the sentences have been swapped round by mistake. Read it through carefully.

> **From:** Manager, Top Building Services
> **Subject:** Swimming pool repair
> **Date:** 8 October 2012 11:07:25 GMT+01.00
> **To:** Mr Iqbal, Aseef
>
> Dear Sir,
> Secondly, we will replace all tiles, both on the bottom of the pool and around it. We will start by emptying the pool. Finally, we will return to fit the new diving board. As requested, here is our three-stage plan for repairing the school swimming pool.
> Yours,
> Mr I Brick, Manager

**a)** Which is the topic sentence in this email? Find the sentence which starts things off, and leads on to the others. Write it here:

...................................................................................................................................

**b)** Now write out the email in the correct order below:

*Dear Sir,*

...................................................................................................................................

...................................................................................................................................

...................................................................................................................................

## LINKING IDEAS USING CONNECTIVES

When you link ideas, sentences or paragraphs, **connectives** can be very useful.

> Here are some of the main types of connectives:
> - Time order (chronological) and sequence: e.g. *at first, initially, later, then, next, finally*
> - Cause and effect, logical steps: e.g. *therefore, consequently, so that, as a result*
> - Development of ideas, or addition of new ideas: e.g. *also, in addition, moreover*
> - Contrasting ideas: e.g. *on the other hand, nevertheless, however, in contrast*

**(1)** Join these ideas in or between sentences with a suitable connective using the ones above or similar ones:

**a)** The work by your company was very poor and ............. I am cancelling the contract.

**b)** The stream has completely dried up. ........................., the reservoir it leads into is 60% lower than last year.

**c)** Sam's speech went on for ages! ........................., when it was over, we woke up!

**d)** There are many benefits to electric cars, for example economy. ........................., they still cost a lot to buy.

**(2)** Can you spot the use of connectives in the paragraph below? Circle them and label them: T (time order), L (logical order/cause and effect), D, (development), C (contrast).

> *I am writing to report on the progress made on the new swimming pool.* ——T
> *Firstly, the builders were late and so work did not begin until midday.*
> *Nevertheless, once there, they worked very hard indeed. As a result, the old*
> *tiles were removed rapidly. Moreover, by the evening they had taken all the*
> *water out of the pool and told me work was complete for the day. Yet,*
> *when I went to look at the pool, I noticed there were still some old tiles*
> *lying around on the grass. In the end, I called the manager and after a while*
> *someone came back to sort things out.*

**(3)** Imagine you are one of the builders. You have to write an official explanation to your boss – the manager of Top Building Services – explaining why you were late. Here are some possible reasons:

- traffic
- oversleeping due to tiredness because of work
- taking children to school
- an unforeseen event

Use the connectives in the box at the top of the page to help you recount what happened. You could start your email like this:

> Dear Mr Iqbal,
>
> First of all, I wish to apologise for being late for work yesterday.

**TOP TIP** Adverbs such as *fortunately* or *surprisingly* can also help you 'signpost' your account of events in informative texts such as this.

SECTION 2: WRITING FOR ACCURACY

## STRUCTURING PARAGRAPHS

**1** Read these notes about Pelé, a famous footballer. They need to be turned into two paragraphs. Remember, a paragraph is usually about one main idea or several linked ideas.

First, decide which notes fit which paragraph: Paragraph 1= Pele's background and early life; Paragraph 2 = Pele's successes as a footballer and his life now. Write P1 or P2 next to each of the notes below.

Edson Arantes do Nascimento is a famous footballer.

He scored 1281 goals in 1363 games.

He was born in poverty.

He played with a sock stuffed with newspapers.

He is better known as Pele.

He is the top scorer of all time.  *P2*

He could not afford a football.

He became very wealthy.

He was born in Brazil.  *P1*

He is well known for supporting causes to improve the social conditions of the poor.

He dedicated his 1000th goal to the poor children of Brazil.

**2** Now that you have decided which points will be in your two paragraphs, turn the notes into sentences which are joined together.

- You could use: *who, which, because, so, although, since, where, when* – or any other connectives.
- You could change the order of the ideas, miss out words or phrases, or rephrase ideas.
- Try to have as much variety in your sentence structures as you can.
- Make sure you include a topic sentence.
- Check that you have written complete sentences. Each sentence must make proper sense and start with a capital letter and end with a full stop.

You could begin your paragraphs like this:

Paragraph 1 – *Pele's early life was difficult ...* (then write about his difficulties)

Paragraph 2 – *Despite this difficult start, Pele went on to be successful.* (then write about his successes)

Notice the link between the first and second paragraph. The phrase *Despite this difficult start* refers back to the previous paragraph *and* leads the reader neatly into the next paragraph.

> **TOP TIP** You could start Paragraphs 1 and 2 with other phrases, such as:
> *In his early life ... In later life ...*
> *As a child ... When he was an adult ...*

## PARAGRAPHS WITH VIEWPOINTS AND REASONS

The best writing allows the reader to follow information or an argument clearly. Read this short opening paragraph to an article in a student magazine.

> I strongly believe that my parents should increase my pocket money. This would encourage me to work harder, and I wouldn't need to go to them every time I needed cash for the bus, to go to the cinema or to meet my friends at the café. These friends, who all get more than I do in terms of pocket money, agree with my point of view. When we are chatting together, we all discuss how parents should really value their children. They are precious after all. So give them more!

**1** Answer these questions:

**a)** What does the topic sentence tell us is the viewpoint of the writer?

It tells us that.............................................................................................................

**b)** What does the demonstrative pronoun, 'this' refer to at the start of the second sentence?

...........................................................................................................................

**c)** Who are the 'who' referred to in 'who all get more than me …'?

...........................................................................................................................

**d)** Who does 'we' refer to in 'we all discuss …'?

...........................................................................................................................

**e)** Who does 'them' refer to in the last sentence?

...........................................................................................................................

Now read the following paragraph, which contains a viewpoint on a separate issue. Here, the writer starts with a general point and includes more and more detail to be persuasive.

> Our holiday on the island was wonderful for many reasons. Firstly, the — weather was great, our room was comfortable and clean and the hotel staff were very helpful. The young man on the desk even telephoned a local jeweller when my wedding ring broke and arranged for it to be repaired. —

*topic sentence*

*builds on main idea, giving further details why holiday was good*

*specific detail elaborates on one of the points in the second sentence*

**2** Answer these questions.

**a)** What is the viewpoint of the writer?

The writer's viewpoint is that.........................................................................................

**b)** What three specific details are given in the second sentence about the holiday?

Detail 1: ............................................................................................................

Detail 2: ............................................................................................................

Detail 3: ............................................................................................................

**c)** What even more specific detail, building on the second sentence, appears in the last sentence?

The specific detail mentioned is: ...................................................................................

...........................................................................................................................

**3** Now have a go at adding more detail for yourself. Read the start of this account about a terrible holiday.

*Our city break was dreadful for many reasons. For a start, the weather was foul, our room was dirty and small, and the hotel staff were rude and unhelpful.*

**a)** Underline the three reasons in the second sentence why the city break was so bad.

**b)** Now choose one of the details from this second sentence and write a third, even more specific sentence, as in the example about the island holiday.

Write the final sentence here.

..................................................................................................................

..................................................................................................................

**4** Imagine the above text comes from a letter to your sister or brother about your dreadful holiday. Plan two further paragraphs about other bad things about the holiday:

Paragraph 2 could be about your problems on arrival. Write down three possible problems:

**A:** The plane was late ....................................................................................

**B:** ..................................................................................................................

**C:** ..................................................................................................................

Paragraph 3 could be about your problems at the hotel. Write down three possible problems:

**A:** The swimming pool had no water in it, and ..............................................

**B:** ..................................................................................................................

**C:** ..................................................................................................................

Use the photos below to give you ideas.

**5** Write the whole letter on a separate piece of paper. Use everything you have learned about topic sentences, linking sentences, joining paragraphs and linking ideas.

## LINKING OPINIONS WITH EVIDENCE

When you argue a point of view, your paragraphs can build towards a powerful conclusion. You could begin with one argument and then add to it with new points. By the end you will have a case that no one could argue against!

Look at these arguments *for* an education system with no tests or exams:

**A:** Tests and exams make students anxious and worried.

**B:** Exams are boring; students could be doing fun stuff!

**C:** Tests and exams only measure a small range of skills.

**D:** Tests and exams waste teachers' time as they have to spend hours marking them.

**1** Look at the examples below. They all provide evidence to support one of the points of view (A, B, C or D above). Circle the correct letter.

| | | | | |
|---|---|---|---|---|
| *Our teacher, Mr Voronin, spent two nights marking our exams. This meant he didn't have time to prepare our lesson, so we just watched a video.* | A | B | C | D |
| *I never sleep well before exams.* | A | B | C | D |
| *Our science exam was two hours long. There was no way it covered every scientific process in the world.* | A | B | C | D |
| *You don't see many students smiling and looking happy in exams. My friends often seem to be staring out of the window wishing they were somewhere else.* | A | B | C | D |

Connectives can be used to link the points and the evidence where needed. You could use the following words and phrases to do this:

> *for example, such as, in this way, because, so, as a result*

**Or sometimes**: *which explains why …, that accounts for ….*

Take this example:

> *Exams give you vital information about your progress. **For example,** after my maths exam, I could see clearly that I needed to practise using percentages as that was the part of the exam I did least well in.*

**2** Now write your points here using a connective word or phrase. You can make one longer sentence or keep the sentences separate.

**A:** Tests and exams make students anxious and worried .............................................................................

**B:** .............................................................................................................................................................

**C:** .............................................................................................................................................................

**D:** .............................................................................................................................................................

## GOING FURTHER

**3** On a separate sheet of paper, write a short article of 100–150 words for a teen magazine about how exams make students feel. You can decide whether you want to focus more on the negative or positive feelings students have.

# ❸ Vocabulary

## SYNONYMS

A **synonym** can help you put other people's ideas into your own words. But synonyms do not always have exactly the same meaning as one another. For example, there are many words in English which mean 'the place where people live', but each word has a slightly different meaning.

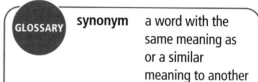

**GLOSSARY**    **synonym**    a word with the same meaning as or a similar meaning to another

See Section 6 for more synonym practice.

Look at these synonyms for 'home':

*slum    palace    bungalow    flat    residence    shack*

Would you know when to use each of the above? Use a dictionary if necessary to find out.

**1** Where would each of these people live? Find a word from the list above:
- a prince
- a very poor person in a city living close to many others
- an average person who lives on their own
- a very poor person living out of town
- an important official
- an older person who cannot climb stairs

**2** Here are some groups of synonyms. Write each set of words in order, from a mild feeling to the most powerful feeling. You can use a dictionary to help you. Sometimes the order will be a matter of opinion, not fact!

**a)** afraid    alarmed    nervous    panicky    terrified    scared    petrified

.................................................................................................................................................

.................................................................................................................................................

**b)** grief-stricken    sad    unhappy    miserable    depressed    distraught    tearful

.................................................................................................................................................

.................................................................................................................................................

**c)** happy    pleased    ecstatic    contented    delighted    positive    cheerful

.................................................................................................................................................

.................................................................................................................................................

**3** Produce another list of synonyms connected with feelings (e.g. *worried, angry*) and order them from 'mild' to 'very strong'. You could type or write them in larger or darker font and print them out as a visual revision check.

## GOING FURTHER

### 'NICE'

There is one nice little word in English which is really useful. And there are times when this little word is just the right word to use. But often this nice little word needs to be taken out and replaced because it is so overused it has lost any real meaning.

**4** Read the following paragraph and underline all the uses of 'nice' in it.

*My friend Luis is very nice to me. He and I had a nice time last Saturday when he took me to the nice burger bar in that nice shopping mall near us. It's really nice inside. Everything is nice and clean and it looks so nice and smart. And the food smells nice, too. And the taste! Well, the burgers we had looked nice and tasted nice. Luis paid for all we had, including an extra big nice milkshake. He really is nice.*

**5** Rewrite the paragraph choosing words from the box to replace each 'nice' you have underlined. If you can think of different words instead, use them.

| generous | fantastic | smart | well-designed | modern | fresh | up-to-date |
| delicious | appetising | scrumptious | kind | creamy | | |

............................................................................................................................

............................................................................................................................

............................................................................................................................

............................................................................................................................

### 'SAY' AND 'GO'

'Say' and 'go' are two other words which we can often replace to express our ideas in a more exact and subtle way. The following exercise will help you use a wider vocabulary.

**6** Read these sentences out loud. Then write which version tells you the most and suggests a story to you, and why.

**A:** 'It's my fault,' she said as she went out of the room.

**B:** 'It's my fault,' she whispered as she ran out of the room.

**C:** 'It's my fault,' she shouted as she staggered out of the room.

The version which gives the most information, and suggests a story is ...........................

because ....................................................................................................................

**7** Then write two more versions of the sentence which you might find in a story.

**a)** 'It's my fault,' she ........................... as she ........................... out of the room.

**b)** 'It's my fault,' she ........................... as she ........................... out of the room.

## USING BETTER VOCABULARY

It is important to learn and use a range of words connected to a particular subject or area. This can be helpful when you are writing a report or arguing a point of view on a particular topic.

**(1)** Group the words or phrases in the box under the headings below. Are there any which go under more than one heading?

| Building | Football | Cookery | Fashion |
|----------|----------|---------|---------|
| .......... | .......... | .......... | .......... |
| .......... | .......... | .......... | .......... |
| .......... | .......... | .......... | .......... |
| .......... | .......... | .......... | .......... |
| .......... | .......... | .......... | .......... |
| .......... | .......... | .......... | .......... |
| .......... | .......... | .......... | .......... |

> design   architect   style   measure   trend   vintage   level   heat
> goalkeeper   simmer   door   line   make-up   accessory   elevator
> football   foundation   pot   red card

**(2)** Choose the correct word or phrase from the box to fill in the gaps in the article.

Many new buildings these days may look modern on the outside, but their interiors have a definite ..................................... feel.
This retro ..................................... has become very popular in both architecture and fashion.  There is a ..................................... to wear ..................................... from the 1950s, particularly bright red lipstick and pale .....................................
One sport that never goes out of fashion is .....................................; the game is more popular than ever. The worst thing that can happen in a game is for the ..................................... to be given a ..................................... and told to leave the pitch.

**(3)** Write the final paragraph for the article using the remaining words from the box.

## GOING FURTHER

There is a problem of too much traffic in your local town and the town council is considering setting up a 'congestion charge'. This means that anyone who wants to drive their car into the town centre will have to pay a sum of money to do so. You decide to write a letter to the council to give your views.

**(4)** First, read this argument that was made at a meeting called to discuss the proposal:

Thank you for giving me the opportunity to speak to you at this public meeting. I feel

badly that it would be very bad to set up a congestion charge for anyone driving a

car into the town centre. It will be especially bad for the people who need the council's

support the most. Many people won't be able to pay the charges. It will be very bad for

people who live in bad areas without buses or trains to get them into town. They need

their cars to get themselves into the town centre. Shopping can be very heavy — how are

they meant to get heavy things to the car parks outside the town centre? The elderly will

be very badly affected. They can't be expected to walk all the way into town. The same

goes for parents with heavy pushchairs and energetic young children. They need their

cars to get into the centre as quickly as possible.

Replace each of the underlined words with one of the words below to make the writing more varied and more precise. Write the letter (A to J) above each underlined word.

**A** travel           **F** afford

**B** passionately     **G** wrong

**C** transfer         **H** unjust

**D** transport       **I** unfavourably

**E** remote         **J** unfair

You may need to check the meaning of some of the words in a dictionary.

**(5)** Now write a short letter to the council giving your own views.

# ④ Clear communication

## TYPES OF PREPOSITIONS

Prepositions are often short words or phrases that tell us how things relate to each other, or the position of things or people. For example:

- single-word prepositions – *at, over, near*
- two-word prepositions – *ahead of; instead of; next to*
- three-word prepositions: *by means of; in front of; in spite of.*

Prepositions often indicate:

- time – ***at** five o'clock; **after** the match*
- position – ***on** the head; **in** the street*
- direction – ***to** the school; **up** the hill*
- means – ***by** train.*

**①** Complete these sentences using an appropriate preposition:

**a)** Are you going ..................................... the music festival?

**b)** Make sure you keep your little brother ..................................... your side at all times.

**c)** We can get to the festival ..................................... bus and then go ..................................... the entrance to collect our tickets.

**d)** It was so exciting! I cried tears of joy when Rihanna came ..................................... the stage.

**e)** I ran ..................................... the front to get a better view.

**f)** ..................................... the show, we got ice cream and lemonade. ..................................... midnight Dad picked us up.

**②** **a)** Underline the prepositions in the paragraph below.

   **b)** Decide which type of prepositions they are and write them under the headings below.

> It all happened during the party. Someone had put too much chilli in the pasta for a laugh, and we were soon coughing and sneezing! I knocked my fizzy drink off the table and someone slipped on the sticky mess. At school the next day, in the lunch break, we found out who was responsible – Ana. She'd had to leave the party early, before nine o'clock, because she was going home by bus, so she hadn't seen the chaos she'd caused.

| Time | Position | Means |
|------|----------|-------|
| .................. | .................. | .................. |
| .................. | .................. | .................. |
| .................. | .................. | .................. |

## USING PREPOSITIONS

Your teacher has said that your class can have an end-of-term party. Your friend, Neve, has been given the job of organising the room. But on the day of the party she is ill, so she sends you the email below:

Hi,

The tables need to go over the windows at the left-hand wall. Place the paper plates next to the table in piles so people can pick them up as they come out. Knives and forks need to be put beyond the plates. When people arrive, give them a plastic glass when they come over the door.

Decorations need to be hung across each corner of the room so they meet in the top of the classroom. While people are eating, make sure that there are no spilled drinks under the floor.

**1** Make sense of this email by replacing the incorrect prepositions with the correct ones listed below:

*on (×2)   in (×2)   next to   as   at   from   under   while   through*

**2** Neve wants to know how the party went. Unfortunately, it was a bit of a disaster. Complete this email back to her explaining what happened:

**To:** Neve

Hi Neve,

Just writing to tell you all about the party. Unfortunately, it didn't go too well ............

.................................................................................................................................

.................................................................................................................................

.................................................................................................................................

.................................................................................................................................

Use as many of these prepositions as you can. You can also make use of the word bank below.

*over   under   through   next to   for a start   after a*
*while   later   above   near   apart from   by*

**Word bank:** *spilled, smashed, fizzy, crisps, kiwi fruit, cheese sticks, pizza slices, window, mop, cloth, unwell, fire alarm, loud, police, music*

## IDIOMS

Idioms are common phrases used by native English speakers, often in the form of similes or metaphors. For example, 'it's bucketing down' describes heavy rain and does not mean that 'buckets' are being tipped out in the sky above!

**(1)** Can you find some well-known idioms in the following texts? What do they mean?

> My sister is always very busy and often bites off more than she can chew. For example, as well as having a full-time job, she runs a football club in her spare time. For this reason, she can sometimes seem very cross and shouts at the children when they are playing football, but her bark is worse than her bite as she is really a very kind person.

> Tom hates parties and dancing, so when his brother suggested having a disco for Tom's birthday, the idea went down like a lead balloon. To add fuel to the fire, Tom went ahead and organised a surprise party anyway, which Tom left immediately.

**(2)** Now read this dialogue between two business people. What are they talking about?

**Jo:**     OK, Steve. For this meeting, we need to remember what we agreed last night so that we are singing from the same hymn sheet.

Meaning:  OK, Steve. For this meeting, it is important that you and I ......................................

................................................................

**Steve:**   I agree. If we play our cards right, it'll be a piece of cake.

Meaning:  If we ...........................................................................................................

**Jo:**     Yeah – dead easy.

Meaning:   I agree, it will be ..............................................................................................

> **TOP TIP**   The best use of idioms is to include them occasionally in your writing. If you use them too much, they begin to sound unnatural.

**(3)** Write the opening two to three paragraphs of an article about the best way to deal with feeling low or sad. You could consider:
- outdoor activities
- talking to friends or family
- meditation or other relaxation methods.

Try to use three or four of these idioms in your writing or any others you can think of.
- *Run out of steam* – to no longer have the energy to continue doing something
- *The last straw* – the last problem in a series of problems that finally makes everything unbearable
- *Under the weather* – slightly ill
- *To be on cloud nine* – to be very happy
- *Wear my heart on my sleeve* – to show my emotions openly to everyone
- *Every cloud has a silver lining* – there is something good even in a bad situation
- *Recharge your batteries* – get back your energy again
- *Fresh as a daisy* – not tired and ready to do things.

Start with:

When I'm feeling under the weather or .................................................................................................................

........................................................................................................................................................................

........................................................................................................................................................................

........................................................................................................................................................................

........................................................................................................................................................................

........................................................................................................................................................................

........................................................................................................................................................................

........................................................................................................................................................................

## COMPARATIVES

The two most common ways of comparing things are as follows:

*Let's watch the football match at home. It's **cheaper**.*

*Don't go to the stadium. It's **more expensive**.*

We tend to use -er for short forms, for example: *fast – faster, big – bigger.*

We also use -er for two-syllable words that end in *y* (the *y* changes to *i*), for example: *tasty – tastier, funny – funnier.*

We tend to use *more* for longer **adjectives**, for example: *more spacious, more interesting, more humorous.*

We also use *more* with **adverbs** that end in *ly*, for example: *more quickly, more carefully, more thoughtfully.*

You can use *than* after comparatives, for example: *It's cheaper **than** going to the stadium.* Or: *Going to the stadium is more expensive **than** watching it at home.*

> **TOP TIP** Remember that there are exceptions when forming comparatives that need to be learned: *good/well/better, bad/badly/worse,* etc.

**(1)** Complete these sentences using a comparative form (e.g. *older, more spacious*).

**a)** That film last night was so boring. Can't we see something ........................................... tonight?

**b)** That pizza was incredibly cheap. I expected it to be ...........................................................

**c)** This homework is very difficult. I expected it to be ...........................................................

**d)** You hardly ever walk with me to school. Why don't you walk with me ........................... ?

**e)** It's a shame my best friend has moved so far away. I wish he lived ....................................

**(2)** In this letter, Rafa is writing to a friend about last year's school tennis tournament. Add the comparatives from the box below to complete the letter.

Dear Roger,

Remember how awful last year's tournament was? I hope this year's is ........................................
................................................last year's. That weather! All that rain! It was quite light to start,
but then it got ........................................ and ........................................ I needed an umbrella!
I won my first match easily, but the second was a real struggle. Andy hit the
ball ................................................................................................ me. That's why I almost lost. I need to
play ........................................Then my game would be ........................................
Anyway, let's hope the sun shines and it is ........................................ this year.
I hate playing in the cold.

See you there!

Rafa.

| heavier | warmer | heavier | harder than | stronger | better than | better |
|---------|--------|---------|-------------|----------|-------------|--------|

## USING COMPARATIVES AND SUPERLATIVES

You can use *a lot, much, far* (meaning 'more'), *a bit, a little, slightly* before comparatives. For example:

*How was work today? <u>Much better</u>, thanks!*

*This homework is <u>slightly easier</u> than yesterday's.*

*This homework is <u>far easier</u> than yesterday's.*

*Some people say that learning Japanese is <u>far more difficult</u> than learning English.*

You can also use *any* and *no* + a comparative:

- *The door is stuck. I can't push it any harder.* (Meaning: *That is the hardest I can push it.*)
- *I expected their garden to be very big. But it's no bigger than ours.*

**(1)** Use the words in brackets to complete the following sentences:

**a)** I enjoyed our trip to the art gallery. It was ........................................ I expected. **(far/interesting)**

**b)** This car is too small. I need something ........................................ **(much/big)**

**c)** I thought she was slower than me, but in fact she's ........................................ **(slightly/quick)**

Use *any* or *no* + a comparative to complete these sentences:

**d)** Raj had waited long enough. He wasn't going to wait ........................................

**e)** The weather isn't particularly bad today. It's ........................................ than normal.

**f)** I'm sorry the music is so quiet. I can't make it ........................................

When using superlatives, we follow similar rules as for comparatives. We add -est for short words (usually adjectives) or *the most* for longer words. For example:

*high – the highest*    *quick – the quickest*    *great – the greatest*

*difficult – the most difficult*    *comfortable – the most comfortable*

## GOING FURTHER

(2) Here is some data about three tall buildings.

|  | Eiffel Tower, Paris | The Shard, London | Burj Khalifa, Dubai |
|---|---|---|---|
| Height | 320 metres | 310 metres | 828 metres |
| Age | Opened 1889 | Opened June 2012 | Opened January 2010 |

Write a short magazine report about famous tall buildings of the world. You could write about their age and height, comparing them.

Three world-famous buildings are the Eiffel Tower in Paris, the Burj Khalifa in Dubai and the Shard in London. The Shard is tall, at ..............................................metres, but the Eiffel Tower is ............................................ at ............................................... metres. However, it isn't as ..................................... In terms of age, the ........................................... of the three is ...........................................

## PREFIXES

An easy and quick way to find the opposite of an **adjective** is to add a negative **prefix**. The most common are: *un, in, im, non, dis* and *mis*.

> **GLOSSARY**   **prefix**   a letter or letters, e.g. 'un-', 'ex-', that can be added to the beginning of a word to form a different word

So a *caring person* becomes an ***uncaring person*** if they treat someone else badly.

These general rules may help you decide which prefix to use, but there are exceptions:

***im*** before a word beginning with *m* or *p* – ***immature***

***ir*** before a word beginning with *r* – ***irrational***

***il*** before a word beginning with *l* – ***illiterate***

**1** Can you add the correct prefix to the words below?

**a)** *inconvenient*  
**b)** ........loyal  
**c)** ........kind  

**d)** ..........patient  
**e)** ..........possible  
**f)** ..........real  

**g)** ..........fit  
**h)** ..........logical  
**i)** ..........secure  

**j)** ..........polite  
**k)** ........fair  
**l)** ........organised  

Some of these prefixes, especially *dis* and *mis*, can also be used with some **verbs**. So:

*My mother **approved** of my choice of car; my father **disapproved** – he thought it was too expensive.*

**2** Now use the words above to fill in the gaps in the following sentences.

**a)** My sister's bedroom is a real mess and she can't find her school books anywhere; she is really ...........................................

**b)** I've started going to the gym every day as I am really ...........................................

**c)** In some countries it is considered very ........................................... to not finish a meal.

**d)** Swimming with dolphins was so amazing, it seemed ...........................................!

**e)** I never talk about my friends to other people, that would be very ...........................................

**3** There are many other prefixes which alter or add to the meaning of words. For example: co- (meaning 'with/together') as in *co-operate*; re- (meaning 'again'), ex (meaning 'former/before') and inter (meaning 'between').

Add the correct prefix to the sentences below. You should be able to work out which one is needed from the context:

**a)** The teacher told the student to ..........write his report.

**b)** The Olympic Games represents ..........national sport at its finest!

**c)** That bridge is so huge it has to be ..........painted every year.

**d)** Both Tim and Jose were interested so in the end they decided to ..........produce the film together.

## USEFUL PREFIXES

Knowing the meaning of some common prefixes is also very helpful when reading texts, especially those with numerical or factual information. Some typical ones include:

*uni* and *mono* (one)      *bi* (two)      *tri* (three)      *semi* (half)      *multi* (many)

**1** Can you work out the meaning of the underlined words from the context of the sentences?

**A:** There was <u>universal</u> agreement for the plan. <u>Unicycles</u> would be bought for all the students!

................................................ and ................................................

**B:** His voice was very boring and <u>monotonous</u>.                  ................................................

**C:** His father is Spanish and his mother is
Portuguese, so he's <u>bilingual</u>.

...................................................

**D:** Slice an orange and cut the slices into <u>semicircles</u> to
decorate the cake

...................................................

**E:** The company used to be based in South Korea and it sold to local people,
but now it's a huge <u>multinational</u> organisation.

...................................................

**F:** Soldiers and nurses wear <u>uniforms</u>; teachers don't.

...................................................

**G:** She was only <u>semi-conscious</u> immediately after the fall,
but by the time the nurse arrived she was fine.

...................................................

## GOING FURTHER

Prefixes are used to build or even create new word meanings: for example,
*preview* = *pre* (before) and *view* (watch) meaning 'to watch something before
everyone else does', usually to give an opinion – like a television critic.

(2) The text below contains some words with prefixes: groups of letters at the beginning
of the word which change the meaning of the word they are attached to. These
words have been underlined.

Look at each of the underlined words and work out which part of the word is the
prefix and what it means. You may need to do some research to find all the answers.
Then try to think of other words which use the same prefix.  For example:

*Subterranean* = below + ground.

Other words which use this prefix include *subway* and *submarine*

---

*The new <u>heliport</u> has been built on top of the block of flats. <u>Unfortunately</u>,
there is so much fog that the pilots sometimes find it <u>impossible</u> to land
there. In fact, <u>international</u> business people are probably better off staying
at the motel on the edge of town. Of course, one alternative is to get the
Channel Tunnel under the sea between England and France, and then take
the <u>hi-speed train</u>. A rough estimate is that 40% of all visitors would rather
take the <u>subterranean</u> route than fly.*

---

# ❺ Clear punctuation

## SENTENCE PUNCTUATION

All sentences must end with punctuation. Normally, this is a full stop.

*I crashed my bicycle into the wall.*

Of course, you can use other punctuation to change the meaning or tone. For example:

*I crashed my bicycle into the wall!* suggests surprise, shock or drama.

*I crashed my bicycle into the wall?* might be asked as question as the rider finds out what happened to him/her after an accident.

You cannot, of course, end with a comma. You can add further information, but you will still need a full stop when the sentence ends. For example:

*I crashed into the wall, ruining my new bike forever.*

**1** This student has written a short piece about the dangers of cycling in a big city. Unfortunately, he/she has forgotten all the punctuation. Copy and rewrite this text below, putting in the correct full stops, question marks and exclamation marks where needed. You will also need to change some letters to capitals when they are at the start of a sentence.

> It is very dangerous riding a bike in our town in fact it's an absolute nightmare you would think drivers would look out for young people on bikes but they don't are we invisible or something it doesn't take half a minute for drivers to glance in their mirrors but they just don't care I wear bright clothing and make hand signals but it doesn't make any difference drivers, especially lorry drivers, seem to think they own the roads what are the local council going to do about it nothing as usual

## COMMAS AND APOSTROPHES

Remember, **commas** can:

**a)** Separate items in a list:

*I bought fajitas, tomato sauce, onions and fried chicken to prepare for the party.*

**b)** Mark off adverbs, parts of sentences or phrases (often as a way of adding detail or organising your ideas):

*Although I was angry, I didn't say anything.*

*Jose, on the other hand, believes the biggest problem is pedestrians.*

Use **apostrophes** to:

**a)** Indicate possession.

If the 'owner' is singular, the apostrophe goes before the 's', for example:

*Japan's government*

*My uncle's bald head*

Note the apostrophe + s after words already ending in 's': *Dickens's novels*

If the owner is plural, then the apostrophe comes after the 's', for example:

*Managers' problems with their teams*

*Footballers' wives*

Exception: nouns with irregular plurals: *children's, men's, women's, people's*

**b)** Show omission.

The apostrophe goes where a letter(s) has been removed. For example:

*There isn't (is not) much you can do.*

*You'll (You will) be lucky!*

**(1)** Read the following text and then rewrite it, adding commas and apostrophes as appropriate. If you need to change or add any words in the process, then do so.

> Even though it was raining we all went to the beach. Luka brought bread cheese salad and iced tea. Dino however brought nothing which made us all mad. Id brought a snack and so had Shan. Dinos excuse was that he hadnt had time to go the shop. However it didnt matter. Tourists hats were getting blown off so we knew a storm was coming and we left after ten minutes.

....................................................................................................................

....................................................................................................................

....................................................................................................................

....................................................................................................................

....................................................................................................................

....................................................................................................................

....................................................................................................................

....................................................................................................................

## COLONS, SEMICOLONS, BRACKETS AND DASHES

A **colon** can introduce a list that follows a general statement:

*We can be proud of last year: increased sales, more customers and higher profits.*

It can also introduce a new part of a sentence that explains or leads on from the first part:

*She was overjoyed: the bag was exactly what she wanted.*

**Semicolons** are useful for contrasts and comparisons, and can link two simple sentences of equal importance. For example:

*Irina likes table tennis; Shan prefers hockey.*

**1** Read this short article from a school website. Rewrite it adding commas, colons or semicolons as appropriate.

> The new library is wonderful more shelf space an internet zone and comfy chairs for relaxing with a favourite book. The internet zone is already popular the computers are booked up every day. Some students come early to do homework on them others use them once lessons have ended.

..................................................................................................................................

..................................................................................................................................

..................................................................................................................................

..................................................................................................................................

**Brackets** and **dashes** can be used to provide additional information or to make details stand out, for example, when describing a situation or event, or adding a humorous comment:

*We didn't mind hanging around at the beach in the winter (despite the cold) as it was where all our friends went.* Luciano (17)

*Florent told us he'd bought a car – not too expensive – to replace his battered old Ford. It was a second-hand car – but a Ferrari!*

**2** Rewrite the following paragraph using dashes (or brackets) as appropriate for additional information or for text that needs to stand out.

> It was peaceful at night except for the occasional buzzing moth and I slept like a baby. When our guide woke me at 5.30am, I felt refreshed despite the time. Outside, our driver a huge man in khaki shorts waited while we climbed into the jeep.

..................................................................................................................................

..................................................................................................................................

..................................................................................................................................

**TOP TIP** Try to avoid comma splicing: this is a common error where a sentence which should have been split up into separate sentences or linked with another word is mistakenly separated by a comma.

For example: *I went to see a film, it was fantastic.* This could be rewritten as:

*I went to see a film, which was fantastic.*

*I went to see a film; it was fantastic.*

## GOING FURTHER

**3** Write the opening two paragraphs of an article in which you give your views about tattoos. You may find these four comments from students helpful:

> *Tattoos can be very individual, and give you a sense of identity.*

> *I like the idea of tattoos, but only ones that are temporary and can wash off.*

> *Once you have a tattoo, you've got it for life.*

> *I got a tattoo to fit in with my mates as they all have them. We had our football team's name tattooed on the back of our hands. We're all regretting having the tattoos done now as we support another team!*

Try to use the **full range of punctuation**.

You could:

- start with a question: *Do you remember the first time you saw someone …?*
- link two ideas by using a semicolon
- make a point and use brackets or dashes to show extra information or a funny aside
- use a colon to introduce a list.

Check your work as you go along – and afterwards.

....................................................................................................

....................................................................................................

....................................................................................................

....................................................................................................

....................................................................................................

....................................................................................................

....................................................................................................

....................................................................................................

....................................................................................................

....................................................................................................

....................................................................................................

....................................................................................................

....................................................................................................

....................................................................................................

....................................................................................................

....................................................................................................

# Section 3: Writing for a purpose
## ❶ Form, reader and purpose

### FORMAL AND INFORMAL WAYS OF WRITING

It will help you complete your writing tasks effectively if you understand the **form** of a text (the type), the **purpose** (what the text is for) and the **reader/audience** (who the text is for). This will also help you decide how **formal** or **informal** the text needs to be.

> **GLOSSARY**
>
> **formal**     very correct and serious (way of writing or speaking), especially in official situations, using standard vocabulary and grammar
>
> **informal**     chatty or flexible style (of writing or speaking) which uses shorter forms (such as I'd) and more idioms

**1** Read the following text extract.

> Dear Sir,
>
> I am writing with regard to an incident that occurred at one of your shops. Indeed, I wish to draw your attention to the rudeness and unhelpfulness of a member of your staff on Thursday. My friend and I had gone into your accessories shop, 'Bits and Pieces', to enquire whether you sold gloves of different colours (red with white spots for one hand, green with yellow stripes for the other) and your assistant, a Miss Reid, said it was ridiculous to want gloves like those, and I should try the rubbish dump! Miss Reid? More like Miss Rude! As manager, you should make sure that all your staff are fully trained and polite and …

**a)** What would you say is the **purpose** of this text, based on what you have read here? Tick the correct answer.

**A:** to enquire where the writer can buy gloves of different colours ☐

**C:** to explain the good and bad points about the shop ☐

**B:** to complain about the writer's treatment by a member of staff at 'Bits and Pieces' ☐

**D:** to persuade the shop manager to sack Miss Reid ☐

**b)** Who is the intended reader or **audience**?

**A:** Miss Rude ☐

**C:** the manager of 'Bits and Pieces' ☐

**B:** Miss Reid ☐

**D:** the writer's friend ☐

**c)** What **form** of text do you think this is?

**A:** diary ☐    **C:** blog ☐    **E:** letter ☐

**B:** newspaper article ☐    **D:** poem ☐

### GOING FURTHER

**2** Which of these phrases from the letter is the **most formal**, in your opinion?

*I am writing with regard to an incident …*     *red with white spots for one hand …*
*I should try the rubbish dump!*

**3** Here is another formal sentence from the text.

*Indeed, I wish to draw your attention to the rudeness and unhelpfulness of a member of your staff on Thursday.*

Rewrite a more informal version of this sentence. Choose the most informal words you can! (This is just a fun task.) Make use of words and phrases like: *cheeky, unfriendly, tell, I'd, I'm.* You could begin: Right then, ........................................................

## DIFFERENT FORMS AND STYLES

**1** Here are some extracts from different **forms** of texts. Can you match each extract to the correct form?

**a)** A letter to a friend

**b)** A diary entry recounting an emotional experience

**c)** A report of an incident in a local paper

**d)** An article arguing a point of view

**e)** A blog from a trip

**f)** A speech to introduce someone

> **A:** The provision of a new bus route to the school from the town centre is absolutely vital. Up to 80% of traffic near the school is people dropping children off, evidence enough of the need for change.

> **B:** It'd be so cool if you could make it, and Mum and Dad would love to see you again. It seems ages since we've been in touch, and we're dying to see you …

> **C:** Today is Bangkok – I checked into the hotel this morning, 7am. Now I'm sitting in a café while it pours with rain outside, though it's dead hot here. Other backpackers keep on coming in, drenched through.

> **D:** It gives me great pleasure to stand here today. When I was asked to suggest someone to open the new gallery, it was a real honour …

> **E:** Such a shock – I can hardly find the words to describe what happened today; I don't want to make a mountain out of a molehill, but …

> **F:** The whole street was closed for at least five hours as fire-fighters fought vainly to save the carpet shop, belonging to the Manzoor brothers …

**2** Some of the clues to the type of text come from the degree of formality and informality each uses. A report in a newspaper is more likely to be formal, for example. Look at task 1 again and write down any examples of the following features you can see:

**a)** Contractions – *I'll, we'd, don't*

.....................................................................................................

**b)** Shorter, chatty sentences or phrases – *Next stop, London …*

.....................................................................................................

**c)** Slang, or 'teenage-speak' – *cool, fab*

.....................................................................................................

**d)** Idiom: common images used to describe something – *every cloud has a silver lining; he was frozen out of the conversation*

.....................................................................................................

**3** Your local council wants to reduce the number of buses from villages into the town centre. Here are some views about this plan:

- *Money is tight. We need to cut non-essential services.*
- *Older people often don't drive. The bus is their link to life.*
- *People should be encouraged to walk or use bicycles.*
- *Villagers bring vital trade to the town. If they stay at home, they'll just shop on the internet.*

Write an article for your local newspaper giving your views about the issue.

Based on this information, answer the questions below:

**a)** What **form/type** of text do you need to write? ............................................................

**b)** What will be the **purpose** of the text? (Think carefully – there may be more than one.)

............................................................................................................................

**c)** Who are the **readers** likely to be? ............................................................................

**4** How **formal** do you think the text in task 1 will need to be? Circle the correct choice below. Think about the readers – are they friends, family, your community?

*Very informal    Quite informal    Quite formal    Very formal*

**5** One student has begun their response to the task in this way:

<u>Yeah,</u> well <u>it's dead obvious, bro'</u>, that we need to look at all the different views about buses. Because people disagree, don't they? It's not as straightforward as we all think. Like, there's those – like older folks – who need them to get around. Then, there's others who should be getting off their backsides and getting exercise. Take me – I'm really lazy, and I live in a village, so it'd do me good to hop on my bike, break a sweat. Know what I'm saying? Course you do.

Underline any examples of informal words or phrases. The first two have been done for you.

**6** Has the student got the form/type of text right? Which of these does the text seem to be?

    **A:** an email ☐    **B:** the transcript of ☐    **C:** an article in a paper ☐
                            a conversation

**7** Which type of text should it be? ............................................................................

## GOING FURTHER

**8** Write an alternative, more formal, first paragraph for the writing task. Use this prompt to get you started:

The problem of bus provision has led to many different opinions being expressed ...............

............................................................................................................................

............................................................................................................................

............................................................................................................................

............................................................................................................................

**9** You have just visited the new art gallery in your town. In it, there is a very surprising work of modern art.

After the visit, you decide to write an email to your brother/sister, who now lives overseas, describing what you saw. In your letter you should:

- say who you went with
- describe the work of art
- give your opinion of it.

The style and vocabulary you choose will need to match the form, purpose and reader.

You have been told the form – an **email**.

Now, check you are clear about the reader and purpose(s) by filling in the spaces below:

**Your reader:** ...........................................................................................................................

**Purpose:** ...............................................................................................................................

**10** Here are some extracts from students responses to the task. Decide whether each extract is of the appropriate level of formality. Then circle the answer 'yes', 'no' or 'maybe':

**a)** Correct reader?

**A:** You know that new art gallery that opened just after you left?          *yes     no     maybe*

**B:** There is a new art gallery in the town where I live, and ...          *yes     no     maybe*

**C:** I am delighted to inform you about some important news          *yes     no     maybe*
about the art gallery, which you are no doubt aware of ...

**b)** Correct purpose(s)?

**A:** Wednesday. Visited the new cafe at the art gallery. Really          *yes     no     maybe*
great! Spent two hours there, sampling all the different
cakes and candy. Didn't hang around long, as there's this
tennis match I want to watch on television tonight, so ...

**B:** You'll probably remember that a gallery opened a few weeks          *yes     no     maybe*
after you left. Well, I've put off going there as art is not
really my cup of tea. But Leo persuaded me, and he was
right. There was this incredible steel sculpture — it's
basically an upside–down ...

**C:** The new art gallery is open from 10 till 6 every day. Visitors          *yes     no     maybe*
can browse the gift shop, wander around the free exhibition,
or stop for refreshments in the rooftop café. There are a
number of popular works of art, including, 'Boat' by Morgan Z.

**11** Which of the extracts A, B or C is closest to the letter asked for in task 9? ............

**12** Now, on a separate piece of paper, write your letter in response to the task. Use the opening you chose above, or your own ideas.

# ❷ Variety of structures

You can use different sentence and paragraph structures to achieve different effects in your writing. For example, you could use a short final sentence after longer ones to repeat or emphasise the first main point.

*I believe you can never have too many friends. You need friends for every occasion, for example, when you feel low, or for when you want to share good news, or when you want someone to tell you the truth.* **Having lots of friends is great.**

**1** Here is a similar text. Can you add a simple, short, final sentence which has a similar purpose to the ones you have read?

*I really don't enjoy visiting big, busy, indoor shopping centres. I find that the lack of natural light, the crowds, the people fighting to get a bargain, all get too much for me.* ...........................................................................................................

...........................................................................................................

**2** Now read another text.

*I believe you can never have too many friends. You need friends for every occasion, for example, when you feel low, or for when you want to share good news. But most important of all is a friend who will tell you the truth when you need it.* **You need someone who is honest.**

What is the purpose of the short final sentence in this case? Tick the correct answer.

**A:** to add a new point ☐

**B:** to stress or emphasise the first point ☐

**C:** to disagree with an earlier point ☐

**D:** to emphasise the point in the third sentence ☐

**3** Now look at a similar idea extended into two paragraphs, the second one a single sentence.

*I believe you can never have too many friends. Friends for every occasion, for example when you feel low, or for when you want to share good news. But most important of all, you need a friend who will tell you the truth when you need it. Someone who is honest.* **This person may well be the most important person in your life, the person who helps you make good decisions.**

What is the purpose of this single-sentence second paragraph here? Tick the correct box.

**A:** to begin a completely new idea which is unconnected to the previous paragraph ☐

**B:** to take an idea from the first paragraph and develop it in more detail ☐

**C:** to cover all the points again from the first paragraph ☐

**4** Short sentences can be used for different reasons. In the example below, one student describes a working holiday he took on a farm.

The old man watched me from his old wooden stool every morning as I struggled to capture the stray goats and herd them into the rickety pen nearby. He said nothing, and betrayed no emotions as I stumbled here and there, trying to round them up. Then, one morning, he stood up.

Why is the final sentence in this paragraph a short one?

**A:** to draw the reader's attention to a change in the old man's behaviour ☐

**B:** because the student has run out of things to say ☐

**C:** to repeat an earlier point – how the old man keeps on standing up ☐

## GOING FURTHER

**5** What do you think is going to happen when the old man stands up? There are some clues in the text, such as the writer being unable to herd the cattle properly.

Write your ideas here:

I think that ..........................................................................................................................................................

**6** Now write the next paragraph. You could make it a one-sentence one which focuses on the old man and what he does next. Start...

The old man ........................................................................................................................................................

..............................................................................................................................................................................

..............................................................................................................................................................................

> **TOP TIP** Single short sentences are all about making the reader follow your ideas. You can have an impact on what the reader thinks or feels. So use them for dramatic effect (a sudden change or development), to emphasise an idea/event and to develop an idea by adding detail.

## TIME ORDER

If you are recounting an event – a visit, a trip, something that happened to you or someone you know – you would normally tell the events in **time order**.

**A:** *I must tell you about my school trip **yesterday**. I arrived at the gallery at 10am and **then** started to look around. **Eventually**, I came to a room with this incredible sculpture in it – a steel eagle …*

However, sometimes you can change the order around for effect:

**B:** *Imagine this incredible, hanging sculpture made of steel in the shape of an eagle. Well, that is what I saw as I walked into the room at the gallery. We had gone there that morning with the school, but I wasn't expecting much when we first arrived at 10am. We looked around a bit, but I wasn't that impressed.*

**1** On the left below you will see the order of paragraph A. In the box on the right, list the order of the second account (paragraph B) as it is told.

Tells about yesterday, gallery at 10am

Starts to look around

Then, into room, sees sculpture

**(2)** Ines was asked to write an article about 'My secret place' for her school magazine. She decided to write about a secret lake in some nearby woods.

First, she wrote a plan showing the time order of events:

1. When and where I first found 'My secret lake'
2. What it looked like
3. Why I don't go there now
4. Where I go now for time to myself

**(3)** Here is the opening to Ines's article:

I first found my own secret place when I was nine years old. I was with my older brother and sister exploring our local woods when I got lost. I wandered around, and eventually found myself in a clearing. I could hear water …

Here is an alternative opening:

Having a secret place to go to think for yourself is very important. Nowadays, I tend just to go to my room, put my headphones on, and listen to music. But, once, I had my own special, secret place to go …

Both texts work well, but what is the difference between the two? Write your answer below.

The first opening tells us straightaway about ................................................................................................................

................................................................................................................................................................................

The second opening is different because it ...........................................................................................................

................................................................................................................................................................................

## GOING FURTHER

**(4)** Here is a plan that you could use for the article. Add further details of your own. (You do not have to use any of Ines's ideas above.)

**a)** When and where I first found it (time, my age, where, who with – if anyone)

................................................................................................................................................................................

................................................................................................................................................................................

................................................................................................................................................................................

................................................................................................................................................................................

**b)** What it looked like (e.g. description of nature/things I saw there; my feelings/why it helped me)

................................................................................................................................................................................

................................................................................................................................................................................

................................................................................................................................................................................

................................................................................................................................................................................

**c)** Why I don't go there now (when I stopped going there and why, e.g. other kids/I grew up)

........................................................................................

........................................................................................

........................................................................................

........................................................................................

**d)** Where I go now for time to myself (e.g. my room; a new 'secret place')

........................................................................................

........................................................................................

........................................................................................

........................................................................................

Now you have your plan, you can decide which section to begin with. You do not have to start with section a); you could start with section d) for variety. From an older viewpoint, you could look back at your younger self.

Write your article for your school magazine on a separate piece of paper.

Try to include variety in other ways too. Think about using:
- short sentences for effect/drama
- paragraphs of different lengths
- building in descriptive details.

## VARIETY WHEN WRITING TO ARGUE OR PERSUADE

Your school has been offered sponsorship by a big fast food company. It will bring in lots of money to the school, which is desperately short of funds, but in return the company wants to install vending machines in all the corridors and serve its food in the canteen.

Write a letter to your school principal giving your views on this issue.

There are many ways you could start your letter. But first, you need to decide your viewpoint. Choose one of these:

*It's completely wrong – no way!*   *I don't really agree, but...*

*It could work, but...*   *It's a great idea!*

You could begin by expressing your point of view **very strongly** in the first topic sentence:

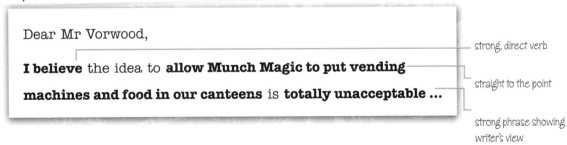

Dear Mr Vorwood,

**I believe** the idea to **allow Munch Magic to put vending machines and food in our canteens** is **totally unacceptable ...**

— strong, direct verb

— straight to the point

— strong phrase showing writer's view

**1** Now write a similar strong first sentence against the idea. Select the strongest verbs and phrases from those provided, and write the new sentence below:

> I (am convinced/am certain/think/wonder if) the idea to allow Munch Magic to put vending machines and food in our canteens is (utterly ridiculous/totally wrong/rather bad/a bit of a mistake).

I ......................................................................................................................

..........................................................................................................................

**2** Expressing your viewpoint so clearly at the start of your letter might not be the best way to persuade your principal. You could begin by mentioning the apparent good points:
- the school needs money
- lots of students like fast food
- new ways of finding funds are important.

So for variety and effect, you could start:

> Dear Mr Vorwood,
>
> I am fully aware that the school needs money, and that ...

Complete the paragraph:

..........................................................................................................................

..........................................................................................................................

Then you could add:

> However, I strongly believe that ...

Complete the sentence:

..........................................................................................................................

..........................................................................................................................

# ❸ Writing notes and short paragraphs

Read this article about falconry and then complete the tasks that follow.

**Falconry** is the act of hunting animals in their natural habitat using a trained bird of prey, often a falcon (a type of hawk), hence the name. A centuries-old activity, it is now mostly used for exhibitions and shows, in which trained falconers let the falcon loose and it returns to its trainer to a range of commands or actions. It can be incredibly dramatic to watch as the falcons swoop down from trees or high in the air to retrieve the morsel of food the falconer offers them.

Phil Wagner has been a falconer for almost 15 years. 'Most people realise that falconry is an ancient sport. But they're fascinated when they see me working with my falcon up close. It's an incredibly close connection between a falconer and his or her falcon.'

Phil explains how the training begins with '**manning**', that is, getting the hawk used to your presence. Once the hawk trusts you as a loyal provider of food and is used to its new surroundings, it will feed calmly on your gloved fist and training can begin. The hawk now has to learn to come to you for food. First, it needs to be attached to a line – called a **creance** – and placed on a post or an assistant's hand. Then, you hold a piece of meat in your gloved fist so the hawk can see it. To start with, it will probably only come a very short distance, but after a few days you can increase the distance to about 50–100m. When the hawk comes this far without hesitation, you are ready to let it fly freely. Then, using a **lure** – a line with meat at the end – you can train it to follow or come to you as you swing the lure in the air.

The specialised words shown in bold go back many, many years – in fact, back to the 16th century. Shakespeare included a speech in his play *The Taming of the Shrew* in which the main character talks about how he is going to tame his wife as if she were a hawk. Not very nice at all!

This just shows that falconry is an ancient sport and remains very popular in many cultures around the world. Many different species of hawk are used, from the Northern Goshawk and Peregrine Falcon, to the widely used Harris Hawk and the Red-Tailed Hawk. In the Middle East, the Saker Falcon is the traditional choice, although Peregrines are widely used, too. The United Arab Emirates is said to spend over 27 million dollars each year towards the conservation of wild falcons. For example, there are two breeding farms in the Emirates, as well as in Qatar and Saudi Arabia.

Medieval falconers often rode horses, but this is now rare, with the exception of a few Eastern European Asian countries. In Kazakhstan, Kyrgyzstan and Mongolia, for example, the Golden Eagle is traditionally flown from horseback, hunting creatures as large as foxes and wolves.

Phil says that people tend to think of falconry as simply an ancient craft which is now only done for entertainment. 'Far from it. My main source of income is not doing shows for people, but actually working with local schools. Many of them are plagued by seagulls, which create mess and nest on school buildings. Every week I visit the schools and Leon, my hawk, drives them away. We don't actually catch the gulls, but our presence is enough to drive them off to find other nesting places.'

① Your school has asked for suggestions for activities at a school open day. You wish to suggest having a falconry display but you need to explain to the School Council what it is.

Make two short notes under each of the headings below.

**What falconry is**

.................................................................................................................

.................................................................................................................

**How falconers train their hawks**

.................................................................................................................

.................................................................................................................

**What hawks are used for apart from for demonstrations**

.................................................................................................................

.................................................................................................................

**2** Imagine you have given your talk to the School Council. Next, you wish to write a short paragraph to remind them of the details of the talk.

Using your notes from task 1, write a few longer sentences about the art of falconry and how falconers train their hawks. You should write no more than 80 words.

## GOING FURTHER

You have been asked to provide a longer written note about falconry.

**3** You will need to read the article about falconry again. Use the following headings to help you plan your written note.

**Falconry in the past**

....................................................................................................................................................

....................................................................................................................................................

....................................................................................................................................................

**How falcons are trained**

....................................................................................................................................................

....................................................................................................................................................

....................................................................................................................................................

**Falconry today**

....................................................................................................................................................

....................................................................................................................................................

....................................................................................................................................................

**4** Now write your note in 100–120 words.

....................................................................................................................................................

....................................................................................................................................................

....................................................................................................................................................

....................................................................................................................................................

....................................................................................................................................................

....................................................................................................................................................

....................................................................................................................................................

....................................................................................................................................................

....................................................................................................................................................

....................................................................................................................................................

....................................................................................................................................................

....................................................................................................................................................

....................................................................................................................................................

# ❹ Writing to inform and explain

When you write to explain something, the most important things are:

- logical structure – using the right verb tenses (e.g. future, present) and choosing appropriate sentence lengths
- clear expression – ensuring your explanation makes sense by choosing the right words and appropriate vocabulary.

Read this text:

*Many children feel afraid of the dark. A child's fear may disrupt their bedtime routine and sleep. There are many ways that parents can help their child to overcome this common fear. A nightlight, comforters such as a toy or teddy and a bedtime routine can help. Take a child's fears seriously but do not pretend to check for monsters as this may suggest to the child you believe monsters could exist.*

**①** Write down the **short topic sentence** that introduces the main idea of this paragraph:

.................................................................................................................................

**②** Write down **three** further examples of **present tense verbs** that show this is an informative piece of writing:

There are many ways .......................................... ..........................................

.......................................... ..........................................

**③** Write down **four** items of **vocabulary** specifically related to children's bedtime used in the passage. The first has been selected for you:

Nightlight .......................................... ..........................................

.......................................... ..........................................

**④** Imagine you have been asked to write an email to a friend who is going on a safari in the African bush. He or she has trouble sleeping, and is worried about the wild animals outside the tent.

From this bank of words, select vocabulary that would be suitable for this email. Then write the words under the relevant headings below.

> **Word bank:** *creatures, camping lamp, torch, book, sleeping bag, mosquito net, insects, shadows, camp leader, jeep, campfire, undergrowth, dreams, friends, lions, sounds*

| Fears | Equipment | People | Sleep | Campsite |
|-------|-----------|--------|-------|----------|
| .......... | .......... | .......... | .......... | .......... |
| .......... | .......... | .......... | .......... | .......... |
| .......... | .......... | .......... | .......... | .......... |
| .......... | .......... | .......... | .......... | .......... |

These headings could form the basis for the paragraphs you write. For example:

Paragraph 1:   fears

Paragraph 2:   people who can help you

Paragraph 3, 4, 5

**5** Now put the paragraphs in a logical order. Would you deal with or mention fears first? Or refer to the campsite? There is no 'right' answer, but you must decide.

**6** Next, select the present tense verbs in these sentences that you might write in the email. Then write the correct version of the verb underneath:

**a)** It is/was a good idea to make sure you zip/zipped the tent up properly.

.................................................................................................................................................

**b)** If you hear/heard sounds outside, didn't worry/don't worry/worried, as most creatures keep/kept away from campsites because of the fire.

.................................................................................................................................................

**c)** You can/were able to help yourself sleep by listening/listened to relaxing music on your MP3 player. Or you can/could just chat/chatted about pop music or television programmes with your friends to took/take your mind off things.

.................................................................................................................................................

.................................................................................................................................................

**d)** If you really can't/were unable to get to sleep, then go/went and sat/sit by the campfire with the camp leader.

.................................................................................................................................................

.................................................................................................................................................

**7** Now write the whole email apart from the last paragraph, using the sentences above or new ones of your own. Write the paragraphs in the order you decided on in task 5.

Dear Istvan,

.................................................................................................................................................

.................................................................................................................................................

.................................................................................................................................................

.................................................................................................................................................

.................................................................................................................................................

### GOING FURTHER

**8** Write the final paragraph of the email to your friend. You could say something about using his torch, or reassure him again about the noises he hears.

Finally, Istvan, you can ........................................................................................................................

.................................................................................................................................................

.................................................................................................................................................

When you write to explain something, it is important to clearly state facts, and express opinions effectively. You should also use the correct tone for the type of writing, for example, a newspaper article will be more formal than an email to a friend but less formal than a letter to your head teacher.

Your parents have asked you to help clear out a room in an older relative's flat. You are not that keen to do it as you do not know your relative very well and whenever you see them they seem really boring. However, when you clear out the room, you find many interesting things and learn a lot about your relative and their life.

Write an article for your local newspaper on the theme of 'not judging someone by first appearances'. Base it on what you found in your relative's room.

**(9)** First, plan what you could write about under these headings:

**Memories of your relative**

........................................................................................................................................

........................................................................................................................................

**The room on first appearance**

........................................................................................................................................

........................................................................................................................................

**Three objects you found that revealed something about your relative**

A: ....................................................................................................................................

........................................................................................................................................

B: ....................................................................................................................................

........................................................................................................................................

C: ....................................................................................................................................

........................................................................................................................................

**Your feelings about your relative after you cleared out the room**

........................................................................................................................................

........................................................................................................................................

........................................................................................................................................

## GOING FURTHER

**10** Now, write your article in 200 words in the space below. You could use:

- **connectives** or other phrases to contrast or compare a change in the way you think about something, for example:

  *I used to think that my uncle was unkind. **However/But/Now** ...*

  ***If** you believe that all elderly people are boring, then you will be surprised by ...*

  ***Despite** how I felt, I was shocked when ...*

- **clear verbs in the present tense** that show your clear thinking now, for example:

  *We **must consider** ...*

  *I **believe that** ...*

# ⑤ Writing to argue a point of view

When you write to present a particular point of view, you need to make lots of points, both for and against the idea.

Imagine you are going to write an article for your school or college magazine giving your views on whether we should preserve endangered species. You have interviewed some experts about the issue and here are some of their comments:

- *Charity leader: 'I think more money is needed to support species under threat.'*
- *Presenter of TV programme on animals: 'People are too obsessed with certain "cuddly" rare animals, that is, rare animals that are soft and cute.'*
- *Warden of National Park: 'If we just allow a species to die out, why will anyone bother to protect the rest?'*
- *Teacher: 'Rare species are important but we must spend money on humans first.'*

Your article should be 150–200 words long.

## GENERATING IDEAS

**1** First, complete this concept map, which includes some of the arguments from the comments above.

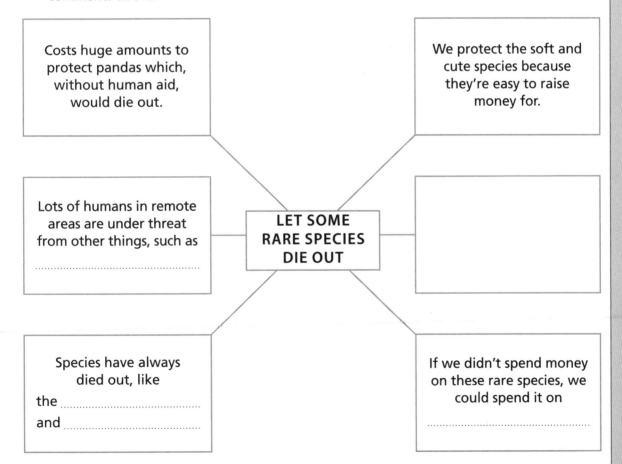

Costs huge amounts to protect pandas which, without human aid, would die out.

We protect the soft and cute species because they're easy to raise money for.

Lots of humans in remote areas are under threat from other things, such as ...........................................

**LET SOME RARE SPECIES DIE OUT**

Species have always died out, like the ........................................... and ...........................................

If we didn't spend money on these rare species, we could spend it on ...........................................

**2** Now complete the concept map on the next page with points *for* spending money on preserving endangered species. You can include the ones from the comments and add your own.

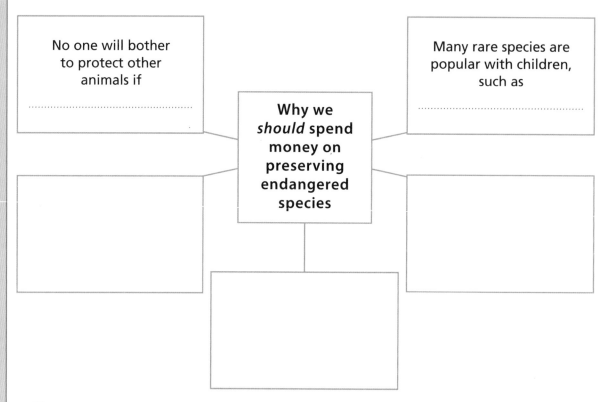

No one will bother to protect other animals if

Many rare species are popular with children, such as

Why we *should* spend money on preserving endangered species

**3** Now you have your points and evidence, you need to build paragraphs. The first paragraph of your article should be quite general. Read these three versions by different students and then write the correct letters in the boxes in a) and b) below.

**Mark**

*It is clear to me that it is wrong to spend money on animals that have little chance of survival naturally. These animals, like pandas, are not suited to modern environments and it is wrong to keep them alive for our pleasure and entertainment.*

**Ayeesha**

*This is, like, totally wrong. The idea that people think we should spend less on rare species is crazy!!! I am completely against it. I love cuddly animals …*

**Ryad**

*The subject of spending on endangered species is a very difficult one, as there are many arguments on both sides. Whether you are an animal lover or not, everyone should have a view on whether we should spend money on preserving particular species or let them die out naturally.*

**a)** Which one(s):

A: introduces the argument clearly and reasonably?

B: sounds balanced and clear on the issues/is not for one side or the other?

C: is not balanced – just expresses one side of the argument?

Ayeesha's ☐        Ryad's ☐        Mark's ☐

**b)** Which one(s):

A: uses appropriate language?

B: uses language that is too informal?

Ayeesha's ☐        Ryad's ☐        Mark's ☐

# LINKING POINTS USING CONNECTIVES

**1** Look at these examples and evidence. Decide which example or evidence leads to the idea or viewpoint on the other side. Draw lines between them.

**Example/evidence**

a) *Rare species like the Yangtze river dolphin died out and no one made a fuss because it wasn't pretty.*

b) *Some animals require lots of land and human help. Without us, they would die out.*

c) *Focusing on pandas, tigers and whales means other areas of nature are ignored.*

**Viewpoint**

A: *We should spend money on species that stand a chance of survival.*

B: *Campaigns should focus more on insects, plants and trees.*

C: *We shouldn't only preserve cuddly-looking animals.*

**2** Now write the linked sentences below using connectives such as:

> *therefore    so    because    as a result*

a) *Rare species like the Yangtze river dolphin died out and no one made a fuss because it wasn't pretty, therefore* .......................................................................

b) *Some animals require lots of land and human help. Without us, they would die out, so* ..........................................................................................................

........................................................................................................................

c) *Focusing on pandas, tigers and whales means other areas of nature are ignored* ......

........................................................................................................................

Next make your own further point using other connectives, e.g. *as a result, this means that, so.*

d) ....................................................................................................................

........................................................................................................................

**3** Now write **three** sentences in favour of spending money on endangered species. Again, use connectives where they are needed.

a) It is important that we preserve animals such as the giant panda ...............................

........................................................................................................................

b) If we don't spend money on well-known endangered species, ...................................

........................................................................................................................

c) Another thing we need to be aware of is ................................................................

........................................................................................................................

> **TOP TIP** Many of these argument-style sentences are about cause and effect. *If we do this, then that …* This is a really useful structure to use in this kind of essay.

## THE END OF YOUR ARTICLE

**(1)** You could end your article by giving your final point of view to your readers. You could choose one of these paragraph starters and then give your viewpoint. Write your final paragraph below.

> *Finally, I believe that …*
>
> *In general, I think it is true that …*
>
> *My final point is that we should …*
>
> *At the end of the day, I feel strongly that …*

...........................................................................................................

...........................................................................................................

...........................................................................................................

...........................................................................................................

...........................................................................................................

...........................................................................................................

...........................................................................................................

...........................................................................................................

...........................................................................................................

## GOING FURTHER

A good argument piece is not just about giving your points and evidence. It must also have an emotional impact, especially if you are trying to persuade your reader. You can do this by adding:

- personal experience or anecdote (this can be made up – it needn't have actually happened to you)
- visual imagery.

**(2) a)** What is the difference between these two students' responses to the task?

**Lia**
*I remember my first visit to a zoo to see a panda. Those huge dark eyes staring out at me, pleading with me. The panda was behind bars like a prisoner. I felt so sorry for him.*

**Luis**
*Pandas are often brought up in zoos in cages and stay there until they die. It is very sad.*

**b)** Underline the personal anecdote in Lia's version and her use of visual details.

**(3)** Now, write your own 'made-up' personal anecdote based on seeing an endangered animal either in the wild or in a zoo. You can choose one of these starters or write your own:

- *It was when I was about five that I first saw …*
- *One day, when I was …*
- *I have a memory that sticks in my mind. My family and I were …*

# ❻ Writing a personal description of an experience

Read how one student describes a terrible journey to a holiday destination in an email home to a friend.

Dear Juan,

We've arrived at last, but I must tell you about our terrible journey![1] As you know, I've been looking forward to this holiday for weeks. Do you remember how I crossed off each date on the calendar as the holiday got nearer?[2] Well, yesterday when we caught the bus to the airport I finally relaxed. One quick bus ride and we'd be on the plane. How wrong could I be?[3]

The bus ride to the airport was dreadful![4] We had roadworks, a demonstration by some students, and even a herd of fat cattle which wouldn't move! I thought we weren't going to make it. Dad spent most of the time beeping his horn and shaking his fist at anyone and everyone. In contrast,[5] Mum sat there very calmly. They're like chalk and cheese![6] Her view is, 'what will be, will be'.

Finally,[7] you'll be pleased to hear, we made it to check-in. As we queued up, I could see the look of relief on Dad's face. At the desk,[8] the assistant looked at us blankly when we handed over our passports and ticket printout. 'Your flight is tomorrow, not today,' she said, pointing to the date on our tickets.

So the truth is I'm writing this email from the airport.[9] We have arrived – just not in the right place! But hopefully, by the time you actually read these words, we'll really be there, sitting by the hotel pool! But for now my bed is a hard, cold plastic chair.[10]

I'll send a postcard or email you when I have some proper holiday news!

Bye for now,

Pavla

---

**①** These are the excellent skills that the student has used. Write the correct number from the text above in the boxes by the descriptions below.

**a)** Short question links to next paragraph ☐

**b)** Topic sentence introduces the idea of the journey and how the writer felt about it ☐

**c)** Clear vivid description helps us **see** the situation ☐

**d)** Connective helps us compare Dad and Mum ☐

**e)** Good use of direct question and 'you' to show this is a letter to a friend ☐

**f)** Sequence word introduces next stage of the personal account ☐

**g)** Preposition helps us picture where this takes place ☐

**h)** Good idiom which shows how different the parents are ☐

**i)** New topic sentence introduces terrible bus ride ☐

**j)** Final paragraph brings us up to date ☐

Note how the **cohesion** in this text is created by each of the four paragraphs: they are about different things, but all linked to the same subject – the awful journey.

GLOSSARY | **cohesion** | the links created within and between paragraphs, particularly by connectives, to make a text flow well

**(2)** Here is a list of possible paragraph titles for the email on the previous page. Four of them are correct.

Select the four titles you think match each paragraph's content in the email and circle 'suitable'.

| A: The nice calendar in our kitchen | *suitable* | *not suitable* |
|---|---|---|
| B: How I was looking forward to our holiday | *suitable* | *not suitable* |
| C: Mum and Dad's wedding | *suitable* | *not suitable* |
| D: An uncomfortable bed for the night | *suitable* | *not suitable* |
| E: The food we ate on the way | *suitable* | *not suitable* |
| F: A mistake at check-in | *suitable* | *not suitable* |
| G: Forgetting our passports | *suitable* | *not suitable* |
| H: An awful car ride with Mum and Dad | *suitable* | *not suitable* |
| I: Why I love airports | *suitable* | *not suitable* |

**(3)** Now write the correct order for the four paragraphs here:

Paragraph 1 ...............

Paragraph 2 ...............

Paragraph 3 ...............

Paragraph 4 ...............

TOP TIP | In personal descriptions, especially ones in which several things happen, the texts are usually linked by time phrases, for example 'finally'.
Real fluency in writing comes when you do not need to repeat words or ideas that you are certain the reader understands or remembers. For example, 'airport' is mentioned in paragraphs 1 and 2 so it does not need to be repeated when 'check-in' is mentioned in paragraph 3.

**4** Write part of a new email from Pavla. She arrived safely at the hotel, but she had a terrible trip to the beach. Describe what happened. Write the second and third paragraphs of that email, following on from the opening below.

Try to use some of the skills you looked at in detail from Pavla's original email.

Dear Juan,

This holiday gets worse! We got to our hotel without a problem, had a good night's sleep and then woke up to lovely sunshine and a nice cool breeze. I know this sounds fine, but wait a moment! Time for a trip to the beach, we all thought, so we took our towels, suncream, some snacks and drinks, and set off.

The problem was ............................................................................

............................................................................................

............................................................................................

............................................................................................

............................................................................................

............................................................................................

............................................................................................

............................................................................................

............................................................................................

............................................................................................

............................................................................................

............................................................................................

............................................................................................

............................................................................................

............................................................................................

............................................................................................

Here are some ideas you could use for your second and third paragraphs, or use your own:

- getting lost
- forgetting something or someone
- changes in the weather
- a silly accident.

Remember: the following connectives will help link your ideas both within and between paragraphs. The main uses are:

- time order sequence – *at first, next, later that day, after that*
- simple ordering of events or actions – *firstly, secondly, finally*
- logical ordering (often related to cause and effect) – *therefore, as a result, because of this, so*
- contrast – *on the other hand, in contrast, however, although*
- development of ideas – *what is more, in addition, moreover, on top of that.*

## GOING FURTHER

You have seen how a really good personal description contains:

- clear, fluent expression – the reader can follow the ideas and events in and between paragraphs
- ideas and events that are linked so they all fit the 'theme' or situation
- clear description – images or things described as if in 'close-up'
- prepositions that help the reader see how things or events are related or connected
- clear paragraphs that each contain different ideas or information, but which are linked by the overall story or description
- a tone or style that fits the form of the text (e.g. email, letter, article).

**5** Imagine that your younger brother or sister took part in a charity fun-run to raise money for your school. During the fun-run something interesting happened.

You have been asked to write an article about it for your school magazine.

In your article you should:
- describe what you saw
- explain how you felt and reacted
- tell the readers what happened in the end.

The photos may give you some ideas, but you are free to use any ideas of your own.

Your article should be between 150 and 200 words long. You can include a title if you wish.

Think about the content of the article and also the style and accuracy of your language.

Now write your article below:

........................................................................................................

........................................................................................................

........................................................................................................

........................................................................................................

........................................................................................................

........................................................................................................

........................................................................................................

........................................................................................................

........................................................................................................

........................................................................................................

........................................................................................................

........................................................................................................

# Section 4: Listening
## 1 Key question words

### QUESTIONING WORDS

Very often, listening questions will include key question words which will help you work out the information you need to give.

> **Where** questions usually mean giving the name of a place, e.g. *the station, Jon's house*.
>
> **Who** questions mean you need to give a person's name or role/job in your answer e.g. *Who has a key for the mystery door? The shopkeeper*.
>
> **When** questions are usually about a specific time, e.g. *2pm, late afternoon, after the show*.
>
> **How many?** relates to a number of people, objects or times, e.g. *How many are going to the show? How many times will Suresh need to visit the hospital?*
>
> **What?** can be linked to time, number or a range of things, so listen carefully for more information.
>
> **Why?** involves looking for reasons, causes or explanations, e.g. *Why did Anya get up early?*

**1** Can you add the correct question word to these typical questions? (At least one of these could have more than one question word.)

a) ........................................... does the bus stop before it reaches Jo's street?

b) ........................................... will the plane take off, morning or afternoon?

c) ........................................... did Raj change his mind about going to the party?

d) ........................................... reason did Soraya give for being late?

e) ........................................... will meet Ben at the end of his round-the-world trip?

f) ........................................... times has Lucy been swimming this week?

**2** Below is the transcript of a short listening exercise. Create five questions using a different question word each time:

**Manesh:** Hi Vijay. Sorry I missed your call – I was out walking with a friend and only just got back. Can you do me a favour?

**Vijay:** Of course. What is it?

**Manesh:** There's no way I can get to the station to pick up Mum at 5pm. Could you get her for me? She said she'll wait by the hot-dog stand.

**Vijay:** I'll take your car. Is that okay?

**Manesh:** No – she's got three large cases so you'll need to take the family car. Thanks!

Write your questions here:

1: ...............................................................................................................................

2: ...............................................................................................................................

3: ................................................................................................

4: ................................................................................................

5: ................................................................................................

## SPOTTING THE CLUES IN THE QUESTIONS

There are usually one or more key words in the questions as well as the 'what', 'where', 'why' ones, which help you decide what you will have to listen out for in the recording.

For example, if the question is: *What is the earliest time you can catch a bus?* You know your answer will definitely be a time. What you want is a *specific* time – so you could underline *earliest time* as a key phrase.

But there are other words too: *you can catch a bus.* It's clear you will need to listen for information about 'buses' and when they leave/depart. You may want to underline *bus* in the question too.

**1** Underline the key words in these three questions:

**a)** How many seats are available for the concert?

**b)** What is the highest peak Shona has climbed?

**c)** When will the café be ready to re-open?

**2** Imagine that you have heard the speaker say:

*The buses give a good service. They run all day until midnight, after the cinemas close. On the other hand, you can catch the earliest one to get to town before the shops open. That bus leaves at 7am.*

Now answer the question:

What is the earliest time you can catch a bus? ................................................................

Sometimes you may hear similar information that you do not need, so take care. Here are some more from the same transcript.

*The buses give a good service. They run all day until midnight, after the cinemas close. On the other hand, you can catch the earliest one to get to town before the shops open. That bus leaves at 7am, but the trains are better; the earliest train leaves at 6.30am.*

**3** A student called Jamie gave the answer: *6.30am.* Why do you think Jamie got this wrong?

I think he got it wrong because he noticed ................................................................

................................................................................................

**4** Now listen to this final text.

Highlight the key words in these questions and then answer them:

**a)** What is the earliest time you can get a tram? ................................

**b)** Which form of transport takes the longest to get to town? ................................

**c)** What time of day or night do the buses stop running? ................................

SECTION 4: LISTENING

88

The audio files for this section can be found at collins.co.uk/internationalresources.

# ➋ Predicting answers, using inference

When you hear short bits of speech on a recording, it will help you if you can work out where the people are meant to be. For example, if you know they are in a coffee shop, be prepared to think of all the vocabulary likely to be linked to coffee shops rather than airports, schools or hospitals.

**(1)** Practise focusing on vocabulary groups by completing this table with possibilities for what you might hear. The first row has been done for you.

| You hear a person say | At least one person is probably in | Some words/phrases that you may hear or need to use |
|---|---|---|
| Shall we have a pizza? | a restaurant or a food takeaway shop | toppings; cheese; cost; delivery service; mushrooms; tomato |
| | a dentist's surgery | |
| Where is your homework? | | |
| | | platform; announcement; delay; on time; waiting room; ticket office |
| | a cinema | |
| | a college or university | |
| | | |

**(2)** When you have finished, add:

**a)** another example of your own to the list in the bottom row

**b)** three extra words to each set of words in the third column.

**(3)** You have practised highlighting key words. Now have another go with these questions. What are the key words in these questions that would help you identify the right details?

**a)** What is the colour of the dress Maria is going to buy?

**b)** How much does it cost to buy a return airline ticket to Moscow?

**c)** In which year was the World Championship held in Istanbul?

**d)** How much did the horse which stood on Erik's foot weigh?

**e)** How far did the young man have to walk through the snow when his car broke down?

**f)** What is the sculpture made out of?

**4** Now have a guess at the answers. You will not *know*, of course, because you have not heard the conversations. But by doing your pre-listening work, you will still be able to have a go and you will see if the *type* of answer you give is correct.

My guesses

**a)** ......................................................................................................................................................................

**b)** ......................................................................................................................................................................

**c)** ......................................................................................................................................................................

**d)** ......................................................................................................................................................................

**e)** ......................................................................................................................................................................

**f)** ......................................................................................................................................................................

**5** Did you have any answers ending with: pounds, dollars, euros, kg, tons, km, miles, yards or metres? Which questions (a to f) could these words be a part of the answer to?

Write the letters here: ................, ................ and ................

**6** Look at some possible guesses below. Write next to each one the letter of the question it could be the answer to. One of them has been done for you.

*1954* ................

*purple with white spots* ................

*stone* ................

*200km* ................

*2 tons* ................

*500 dollars* ................

**7** Now you can test yourself.

Listen to the dialogues once and answer what you can. Then give yourself 30 seconds to check your answers and focus your mind on what parts you will have to listen to extra carefully on the second listening. Then play the recording a second time. This is your chance to double-check your answers and to fill in any gaps.

**4.2**

**a)** What is the colour of the dress Maria is going to buy? ................................................

**b)** How much does it cost to buy a return airline ticket to Moscow? ................................................

**c)** In which year was the World Championship held in Istanbul? ................................................

**d)** How much did the horse which stood on Erik's foot weigh? ................................................

**e)** How far did the speaker have to walk after his car broke down? ................................................

**f)** What is the sculpture made out of? ................................................

SECTION 4: LISTENING

The audio files for this section can be found at collins.co.uk/internationalresources.

# UNITS OF MEASUREMENT

Listening tasks can include some questions where you are asked for numbers and some kind of measurement, such as:

**height/length/distance:** *feet and inches; millimetres, centimetres, metres and kilometres*

**weight:** *pounds, ounces and tons; milligrammes, grammes, kilogrammes and tonnes*

**cost:** *pounds, dollars, euros, dinars, rupees, etc.*

**times:** *am or pm; hours, minutes and seconds*

> **TOP TIP**
> Ensure that you know all these words for measurements and can spell them correctly. Use a dictionary for any you are unsure of. Always include the unit of measurement if necessary, for example: grammes, dollars. If you just give a number, it might not answer the question properly.

**1** Here are some answers to the listening questions you did on the previous page.

Remember that your answer needs to show that you have fully understood what you have heard, so you need to include any relevant details such as units of measurements. Which of these answers includes enough detail to show the listener has understood?

| Question number | The right answer | Sample answer | Does the sample answer show full understanding? Why/why not? |
|---|---|---|---|
| b) | 600 euros | six hundred euros | |
| | | E600 | |
| | | 600 | |
| d) | 700kg (*or* kilogrammes) | 700 | |
| | | 700 kilos | |
| e) | 10km (*or* kilometres) | 10 | |
| | | ten kilometres | |
| | | 10 miles | |

# ❸ Keeping the answers brief

Some listening questions only require a brief answer. So, you need to select the correct details from the text, but not include unnecessary information.

Here are some sample answers to the same questions as the ones you answered.

**Q:** *What is the colour of the dress Maria is going to buy?*

**A:** The red roses on the skirt here are so pretty. But the blue one is definitely more suitable.

**(1)** Why do you think the sample answer says this? Tick the best explanation below.

**a)** The person didn't know the correct answer and so just wrote down anything to do with colour. ⬜

**b)** The person knew the answer but wanted to give extra information for an extra mark. ⬜

**c)** The person didn't understand the question at all. ⬜

**(2)** Here's another sample answer:

The blue one is definitely more suitable. Yes that's the one.

Is this a good answer? Tick the statement you agree with.

**A:** Yes, it's the right answer and could not be improved. ⬜

**B:** Yes, it's the right answer but the person has wasted time by including unnecessary words. ⬜

**C:** No, it's the wrong answer altogether. ⬜

Keep your answers as brief as possible. Here is a similar question from a different text with a correct answer that is brief and to the point.

*What is the colour of the football shirt James preferred?*

Answer: red

**(3)** Here are some answers which contain the right answer from the dialogues you heard. Make the answers brief while making sure you are still answering the question correctly.

**a)** That'll be 600 euros altogether then. ........................................

**b)** About 700kg, the owner told me. ........................................

**c)** I suppose I had to make my own way for 10km – but 5km of that was across country.

........................................

**d)** It's just a shapeless blob – a great lump of glass and plastic.

........................................

## RECOGNISING NUMBERS

Sometimes, you have to be able to recognise numbers to answer listening questions.

Make sure you know and can spell all the main number words.

**1** Close your eyes and point to a cell on the grid below. Then write the number out in words in the space below. Do this at least five times; check your spellings in a dictionary.

| 8 | 10 000 | 1 | 19 |
|---|---|---|---|
| 13 | 40 | 3 | 2 |
| 12 | 14 | 15 | 6 |
| 4 | 17 | 7 | 18 |
| 60 | 5 | 30 | 20 |
| 11 | 70 | 50 | 10 |
| 90 | 100 | 1000 | 80 |
| 16 | 9 | 100 000 | 1 000 000 |

..............................................    ..............................................

..............................................    ..............................................

..............................................    ..............................................

**TOP TIP** Formerly, in English, one billion is 1 000 000 millions. In American English, one billion is 1000 millions. As there is a potential for confusion, you should always write 'one billion' in words.

Practise writing and saying very long numbers, for example: 13 492 is *thirteen thousand, four hundred and ninety-two*. When you have written this down and you are sure it is right, read it to a friend and see if they can write it down as a number.

**2** Now complete this table:

| 1 | first | 5 | | 9 | |
|---|---|---|---|---|---|
| 2 | second | 6 | | 10 | |
| 3 | | 7 | | 11 | |
| 4 | | 8 | | 12 | |

## GOING FURTHER

Now for some extra practice, listen to some numbers and write them down.

**3** **a)** The first time you hear the recording, write the numbers you hear as numerals in the spaces below. Listen carefully – sometimes there is more than one number.

1  2 ...............................................  6  ...............................................

2  ...............................................  7  ...............................................

3  ...............................................  8  ...............................................

4  ...............................................  9  ...............................................

5  ...............................................  10  ...............................................

**b)** On the second hearing, write them as words.

1  two ...............................................  6  ...............................................

2  ...............................................  7  ...............................................

3  ...............................................  8  ...............................................

4  ...............................................  9  ...............................................

5  ...............................................  10  ...............................................

**4** Now listen to another recording and do the same again.

**a)** Write the numbers as numerals the first time you hear the recording.

1  1st ...............................................  6  ...............................................

2  ...............................................  7  ...............................................

3  ...............................................  8  ...............................................

4  ...............................................  9  ...............................................

5  ...............................................  10  ...............................................

**b)** The second time you hear the recording, write the numbers as words.

1  first ...............................................  6  ...............................................

2  ...............................................  7  ...............................................

3  ...............................................  8  ...............................................

4  ...............................................  9  ...............................................

5  ...............................................  10  ...............................................

The audio files for this section can be found at collins.co.uk/internationalresources.

**5** You now have the chance to complete a full practice task.
Listen to the recording and answer the questions as directed.

**4.5**

**For questions 1 to 6 you will hear a series of short sentences.**

**Answer each question on the line provided.**

**Your answers should be as brief as possible.**

**You will hear each item twice.**

1: At what time will Aaron's mother pick him up from the airport?

.............................................................................................................................

2: How much does it cost for two tickets for the semi-final?

.............................................................................................................................

3: Why can't Irina go to the skate park?

.............................................................................................................................

4: How will Peter be able to spot Jen at the music festival?

.............................................................................................................................

5: What three camping items must Andreas bring for the trip?

.............................................................................................................................

.............................................................................................................................

.............................................................................................................................

6: What does the cake look like? Give two details:

.............................................................................................................................

.............................................................................................................................

The audio files for this section can be found at collins.co.uk/internationalresources.

# ④ Listening carefully for details

When you are doing a listening exercise where you have to fill in gaps in a form, always check that your answers make sense.

Read the questions first to decide the type of information you are listening for, so that you can identify the details you need from the text. Make sure you read the instructions so that you know how many words are required in your answer.

This exercise will help you practise this skill.

**①** Listen to the following interview about bees and then complete the details below:

Look at this form and complete the gaps in this form, using **one word** only for each gap.

---

Richard works as a ................................

- Bees are used for producing ................................

- Suffered from many ................................ from the bees.

- Number of bees missing: ................................

- Number of US states where same thing happened:

  ................................

---

**②** Now look at this answer and with a partner decide where you would give one mark, and where you would give zero:

---

Richard works as a *keeper* ................................

- Bees are used for producing *honey* ................................

- Suffered from many *put up with countless stings* ................................ from the bees.

- Number of bees missing: *1000 000 000* ................................

- Number of US states where same thing happened:
  *twenty-four* ................................

---

The audio files for this section can be found at collins.co.uk/internationalresources.

**3** Listen to an interview about a famous cycle race, the Tour de France, and then complete the details below.

GLOSSARY **prestigious** admired and respected

**treacherous** very dangerous

## The Tour de France

**The Tour de France:** a world-famous cycling race that tests people to the limit!

**Where it takes place:**

● Traditionally takes place in France, but some stages in nearby countries such as

  ...................................................

● Goes through towns, cities and ................................................... all over France.
● Finishes in Paris every year.
● Length of tour: ................................................... .

**Teams and riders:**

● About ................................................... riders take part.
● Usually about 20–22 teams.
● ................................................... riders in each team.

**Winners:**

Overall winner wears ................................................... .

The 'King of Mountains' wears ................................................... .

................................................... people have won more than once.

**Conditions:**

Temperatures can be ................................................... and the landscape varies,

with ................................................... and ................................................... .

# ⑤ Listening to monologues

A monologue is a long speech given by one person. The following task is a practice to help you prepare for listening to monologues.

> **TOP TIP**
> - Listen very carefully to each speaker to identify their ideas and opinions.
> - Listen for what is implied but not said directly.
> - Think about what is different about what each speaker says.

**①** You will hear six people talking about work and jobs. For each Speaker 1 to 6,  choose from the list A to G, which opinion he/she speaker expresses. Write the letter in the box. Use each letter only once. There is one extra letter which you do not need to use.

Speaker 1 ☐

Speaker 2 ☐

Speaker 3 ☐

Speaker 4 ☐

Speaker 5 ☐

Speaker 6 ☐

**A:** I am a creative person and like working for myself.

**B:** I love working and my life wouldn't be complete without a job.

**C:** I don't want to get promoted if it means telling other people what to do.

**D:** I am very confident and ambitious about the work I do.

**E:** I much prefer working outside to a job in an office.

**F:** I would like to do a well-respected job, but I am not sure I could handle the pressures.

**G:** I prefer having my independence and being able to relax.

The audio files for this section can be found at collins.co.uk/internationalresources.

## PART A

You will listen to a nutritionist giving a talk about chocolate, and whether it is good or bad for you. Listen to the talk and complete the notes in Part A. Write one or two words in each gap. You will hear the talk once.

**Chocolate and the heart**

Recent research suggests that moderate amounts of chocolate can prevent heart ..................................................

There are chemicals which act as anti-oxidants. These can prevent damaging .................................................. building up and polluting the body.

**The reduction in risk of heart attack**

Eating 100g of dark chocolate per day can reduce the risk by ..................................................

**Other benefits**

Caffeine in chocolate can make you feel more alert.

Other chemicals can create a ..................................................

**Problems**

The high amount of sugar in chocolate can cause ..................................................

## PART B

Now listen to a conversation between two students about whether chocolate is healthy or not, and complete the sentences in Part B. Write one or two words only in each gap. You will hear the conversation once.

**New research:**

Some researchers were concerned that testing the effects of chocolate on people wasn't very reliable.

The .................................................. might be all in the mind.

So they suggested it would be better to have imitation chocolate too and use .................................................. bars that looked like real ones to give people they tested.

**Good advice**

It is best to have chocolate .................................................. a meal.

It is also a good idea to buy .................................................. chocolate as it has less sugar in it.

It is very difficult to leave unfinished chocolate in the fridge.

So buy .................................................. as this means you will eat less, and it won't matter if you finish them.

The audio files for this section can be found at collins.co.uk/internationalresources.

# ⑥ Listening for multiple-choice answers

**①** George, a student, is asking Susie Long some questions about her circus act as part of a school radio programme. Read the questions and then listen to the conversation.

**4.11**

For each question choose the correct answer, **A**, **B** or **C** and put a tick [✓] in the appropriate box.

You will hear the talk twice.

**a)** What sort of events does Susie say she performs at?

**A:** football matches ☐

**B:** music festivals ☐

**C:** birthday parties ☐

**b)** Why did Susie become a tightrope walker?

**A:** Her family were circus performers. ☐

**B:** She wasn't allowed to be a lion tamer. ☐

**C:** She wasn't good at anything else. ☐

**c)** Who is showing signs of wanting to be a tightrope walker?

**A:** Susie's younger brother ☐

**B:** Susie's daughter ☐

**C:** Susie's neighbour ☐

**d)** Susie doesn't use a bicycle in her act at the moment because

**A:** she wants to use a motorbike, like her father. ☐

**B:** she prefers to do handstands. ☐

**C:** she had a fall from a bicycle when she was practising. ☐

**e)** How was Susie cured of her fear?

**A:** By practising and practising. ☐

**B:** She read about a French high-wire artist. ☐

**C:** She went to New York for help. ☐

**f)** How high was the wire Susie crossed in her show in Australia?

**A:** 35 metres ☐

**B:** 20 metres ☐

**C:** 417 metres ☐

**g)** What does Susie do to prepare herself for a show?

**A:** She listens to music. ☐

**B:** She checks the towers on her own. ☐

**C:** She does physical and breathing exercises. ☐

**h)** What new act is Susie working on at the moment?

**A:** diving from a high platform ☐

**B:** swaying on a 25-metre pole ☐

**C:** carrying her daughter on her shoulders ☐

The audio files for this section can be found at collins.co.uk/internationalresources.

# Section 5: Speaking

You don't have to be with other people to practise your speaking skills. Look at these ideas that work for other students of English and try them yourself:

**Shadow speech:** listen to an audio text, like a podcast, and repeat what you hear. If the text is also available, you may find it helpful to read this while repeating the words. After some practice, try repeating what you hear <u>without</u> reading the text at the same time.

**Self-talk:** record yourself giving a speech, telling a story or having an imaginary conversation. Listen to your recording and think about how you could improve it.

**Read out loud:** from a book, magazine, blog, etc. Reading will also help your vocabulary. Words are easier to remember when you see them in context.

**Listen and repeat:** listen to songs and read the words of the lyrics to help; watch English films with subtitles for support if needed; listen to audio books and podcasts.

**Talk to friends:** use any opportunities to speak English, perhaps with friends, family or people you meet who are either English speakers or who are also learning English.

The speaking activities in this section may be used for self-study and homework or to practise with a study buddy online. They can also be used for pair work and group work in class as extension tasks.

# ❶ Keeping calm and speaking with confidence

## BEING PREPARED

> **TOP TIP**  If you feel nervous before a speaking task, this breathing exercise can help you to feel calm:
> 1  Take a long, slow breath in through the nose, filling the lower lungs first and then the upper lungs.
> 2  Hold in the breath for 2–3 seconds.
> 3  Breathe out slowly through your lips, trying to relax the muscles in the face, shoulders and stomach.

To prepare for a speaking exercise, it's a good idea to think about topics that you may be asked to talk about or questions that you may be asked in different situations. You can then prepare and practise your answers in advance to help you feel confident about your responses.

**(1)** Write three questions you might be asked in the following situations:

**a)** In a job interview

**b)** When you're buying a train ticket

**c)** When you meet someone for the first time

Now think about what answers you would give to each of the questions. Practise speaking the answers aloud to yourself, practising them with a friend, or recording yourself.

**(2)** Match the questions and answers below:

**1**  *What are your hobbies?*

**2**  *Do you have sisters or brothers?*

**3**  *Do you live in a town or in the countryside?*

**a)** *I enjoy swimming and listening to music.*

**b)** *I live in a small village in the countryside.*

**c)** *I have one sister and one brother.*

**(3)** Remember that to keep the conversation going, you may be asked more questions or need to give more information. Continue the conversations above with two more points. The first one has been done for you as an example.

*What are your hobbies?*

*I enjoy swimming and listening to music.*

*I swim every Saturday at my local swimming pool and I sometimes take part in swimming competitions.*

*I like listening to music to relax, and I also find it helpful to have music on when I work as long as it's not too loud.*

**4** Now write down points relating to each of these topics and practise your answers:

**a)** Do you like going to museums?

**b)** If you could have any pet that you wanted, what animal would you choose?

**c)** What's your favourite subject at school?

## ORGANISING YOUR THOUGHTS

**1** Imagine you are speaking about the topic *Animals should not be kept in zoos*. Put the following phrases into a clear, organised order.

**a)** I also think it's unkind to keep animals in cages because they don't have enough space and they can't hunt.

**b)** Some people might enjoy seeing animals in zoos but as I said they should only be taken from their natural surroundings for reasons which will help the animals.

**c)** However, there are some situations when it is good to take animals from the wild. For example, for breeding programmes if they are an endangered species or to give medical treatment if they are injured.

**d)** i agree that animals should not be kept in zoos because they should be free to live in their natural environment.

Now read the text out loud, as if you are giving a speech about animals in zoos to your class.

Notice how it can be helpful to organise your thoughts in this order:

● 1st point – state your opinion and the main reason for your opinion

● 2nd point – give a second reason for your opinion

● 3rd point – give an opposing opinion to show that you realise there may be a different point of view. You could start this sentence with "*However…*"

● 4th point – make a final point which confirms your opinion.

**2** Now look at the topics below and think about your views on each question. Choose one of these and write notes to organise your thoughts in the order of the points above.

● *Is living in the countryside better than living in a big city?*

● *If I could have a superpower, what would it be?*

● *Is skateboarding fun or dangerous?*

● *A holiday in the snow or a holiday in the sun?*

Use your notes to practise speaking about the topic you've chosen.

## IF YOU DON'T UNDERSTAND

There may be times when you don't understand what someone's saying, so it's useful to practise phrases to help keep you calm if that happens.

**1** Choose and circle the correct word to complete the sentences.

| | | |
|---|---|---|
| I'm sorry but I ................. understand. | **don't** | **haven't** |
| Please ................. you repeat? | **did** | **could** |
| Could you speak ................. please? | **more slowly** | **slow** |
| I don't ................. what this word means. | **understand** | **understood** |
| Please could you ................. this word? | **explain me** | **explain** |
| Does 'afraid' ................. 'scared?' | **mean** | **is meaning** |

## IF YOU CAN'T FIND THE RIGHT WORD

If you can't remember the exact word you want to use, try using different words or other ways to explain what you want to say. Here are some things you could try:

- **Use a different word:** for example, if you don't know the word 'surgeon', say 'doctor.' If you can't remember 'in my opinion', say 'I think' or 'I believe.'
- **Give an example:** for example, if you don't know the word 'cutlery', you could give examples like 'knife, fork and spoon'.
- **Give a description:** for example, 'it's a person who…' / it's a thing that ….' / 'it's a place where….'
- **Describe what it does:** for example, if you don't know the word 'scissors' you could say 'they are used to cut paper'
- **Use a word with a similar meaning (synonym):** for example, if you don't know the word 'large' you could say 'very big'.
- **Use a word with an opposite meaning (antonym):** for example, if you don't know the word 'weak' you could say 'not strong'.

**1** Practise explaining the following words, using the tips above.

**a)** dentist: is a person who .................................................................................

**b)** ancient: a word with a similar meaning is .................................................

**c)** kitchen: is the room where ........................................................................

**d)** intelligent: if someone is intelligent, it means they are ...........................

**e)** celebration: an example of a celebration is .............................................

**f)** expensive: if something is expensive, it means that it's not ......................

# ② Communicating clearly

## USING A RANGE OF GRAMMAR AND VOCABULARY

Your listener needs to understand whether you are talking about the past, present or future. Using the correct tense is important for clear communication.

**(1)** Circle the correct verb form in each of these sentences. Then read out loud the full, correct sentence.

a) Since the age of 12, **I am interested in/have been interested in/was interested in** the stars and planets of the universe.

b) I **go/went/am going** swimming every day because it makes me feel better physically and mentally.

c) I believe that a plant-based diet is good for the environment so I **am not eating/ don't eat/didn't eat** meat.

**(2)** Finish the following sentences about yourself, remembering to use the correct tense.

- Last year was a good year because ...................................................................................
- So far, today has been a good day because .............................................................
- On Sundays I usually ...................................................................................................................
- Tonight I am going to ................................................................................................................
- If I was given a lot of money, I would ............................................................................

**(3)** Now think of a famous person and imagine what they might say to finish the sentences above.

**(4)** Using the right vocabulary will also help you to express yourself clearly. Write down eight words connected to each of the following topics:

- music
- food
- films
- holidays
- sport
- school
- family
- nature

**(5)** Speak for two minutes on each topic above using the words you have written. Record yourself and tick each word as you use it.

## SHOWING CONTROL OF PRONUNCIATION

There are four main features of pronunciation.

**1** Listen to examples A, B, C and D and match them to the correct feature.  5.1

| A | <u>pa</u>tient / po<u>ta</u>to / combi<u>na</u>tion |
| B | L, R / K, Ch / H / F, TH |
| C | No you <u>can't</u> go to the party. / She <u>hates</u> apples. / My dad bought a <u>red</u> car this time. |
| D | Are you ready to start yet? / Is John leaving on Thursday or Friday? |

| 1 | Sounds |
|---|---|
| 2 | Word stress |
| 3 | Intonation |
| 4 | Sentence stress |

Listen to the examples again and repeat them out loud.

> **Sounds:** Remember that there are both vowel sounds and consonant sounds in English.
>
> **Word stress:** the part of a word which is pronounced stronger, eg. communi<u>ca</u>tion.
>
> **Intonation:** the way your voice rises or falls.
>
> **Sentence stress:** the word in a sentence which is pronounced stronger, eg. she <u>hates</u> apples.

**TOP TIP**
Remember
**SWIS: S**ounds, **W**ord stress, **I**ntonation, **S**entence stress

**2** Have some fun with **sounds** by saying the following silly sentences out loud. Identify the difficult sound or sounds in the sentence. Then put the whole sentence together. Finally, repeat the sentence three times, as quickly as you can.

- Red lorry, yellow lorry.
- I saw a kitten eating chicken in the kitchen.
- Harry the hungry horse is happily eating honey in his house.
- He threw three free throws.

Think about sounds that you find difficult to pronounce and write your own silly sentences to say out loud.

**TOP TIP**
It is always better to say fewer words and pronounce them well than say a lot of words and pronounce them badly.

The audio files for this section can be found at collins.co.uk/internationalresources.

3. Group the words in the box under the headings below. Then say the words out loud to practise the correct **word stress**.

| jobs | hobbies | food and drink | countries |
|------|---------|----------------|-----------|
|      |         |                |           |

> doctor   photographer   to<u>ma</u>to   Aus<u>tra</u>lia   <u>Po</u>land   <u>cho</u>colate
> <u>gar</u>dening   lemo<u>nade</u>   <u>ba</u>sketball   Viet<u>nam</u>   gym<u>nas</u>tics   elec<u>tri</u>cian

Listen to the audio to check your pronunciation. Repeat each word as you hear it.

You can add any other words you can think of that could go in each group. Practise the correct stress for each word.

> **TOP TIP**
> When you look up a word in a dictionary, check the word stress. In some dictionaries, there is a **stress** mark (a symbol that looks like an apostrophe) after the syllable that is **stressed**, in other dictionaries the syllable that is stressed is underlined.

4. Listen to the following sentences and decide if the **intonation** is falling, rising or rising then falling:

- My name is Mohammed.
- What did you watch on Netflix last night?
- Is it cold outside?
- In my free time I love watching TV, playing video games and meeting with friends.
- We need to go home now, don't we?
- That book looks really interesting.

Listen again and repeat the sentences out loud.

> **TOP TIP**
> **Notice when intonation rises and falls in sentences.**
> **Simple statements:** falling intonation.
> **'Wh' questions:** usually falling intonation.
> **Yes/no questions:** rising intonation.
> **Complex sentences:** rising then falling at the end.

5. Write some sentences and questions of your own and say them out loud. Listen to your intonation and check that it rises and falls as explained in the TOP TIP box.

The audio files for this section can be found at collins.co.uk/internationalresources.

**6** Listen to a guide talking to tourists on a trip around the capital of Pakistan.

Does she sound bored or interested – why?

**7** Now listen to another guide giving the same tour.

Answer the following questions:
- Which guide is more interesting to listen to? Why?
- Which of the talks is easier to follow? Why?
- Which of the guides would you prefer to listen to? Why?

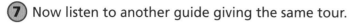

**8** Choose one of these topics to talk about:
- your country
- your friends
- your future plans

Write your talk first and then practise speaking it out loud. Use intonation to make yourself sound interesting. Try not to speak too slowly or too quickly. Remember to pause where appropriate, for example after a comma or full stop.

**9** The meaning of what you say will also change according to which word or words you stress. Listen to the audio and notice how the meanings of the sentences change.

**10** Read each line of the first column out loud, stressing the underlined word when you say it. Then match each one to the end of the sentence in the second column to make the whole sentence make sense.

| **I** am not flying to Canada tomorrow | but I am going to England. |
|---|---|
| I am not **flying** to Canada tomorrow | but my sister is. |
| I am not flying to **Canada** tomorrow | but I am going there on Friday. |
| I am not flying to Canada on **Thursday** | because I decided to take the train. |

Check your answers by listening to audio 5.7.

**11** Write similar sentences and practise saying them, changing the sentence stress each time.

The audio files for this section can be found at collins.co.uk/internationalresources.

# ❸ Expressing ideas and opinions

## GIVING OPINIONS

● Have you ever been on a day trip or longer holiday with your teacher and classmates?

● What are the good and bad things about going away on school trips?

**1** Listen to the conversation between two teenagers who have just come back from a school trip to Paris.

**a)** What was Sara's favourite part of the trip?

**b)** Why did Jon enjoy the picnic?

**c)** Did Jon like the hostel? Why/why not?

**2** Now read the text of the conversation and underline the phrases used to express opinion.

| | |
|---|---|
| **Jon:** | I really enjoyed the trip and I think it was great not having to do any homework. |
| **Sara:** | Well, for me the most exciting part was going up the Eiffel Tower. |
| **Jon:** | To be honest I wasn't very interested in that. In my opinion the picnic was the best because I got to practise my French with different people. |
| **Sara:** | Yes, I liked the picnic too, but mainly because I really feel that food tastes better when you eat it outdoors. |
| **Jon:** | The worst part was the hostel. I guess that that I'm just too old to share a room. |
| **Sara:** | Ha, ha! Anyway, from my point of view we should definitely have a similar trip next year. |

**3** Listen to the audio again and pause it after each person speaks to repeat the sentence yourself. If you're working with a partner, take turns speaking the part of Jon or Sara.

The audio files for this section can be found at collins.co.uk/internationalresources.

**(4)** Jon's teacher liked the idea of going away the following year and asked his class for suggestions. Here are their ideas.

> *A cultural trip, visiting lots of museums and art galleries.*

> *An activity week of playing team games and doing outdoor challenges.*

> *A week practising yoga and meditation and eating healthy food.*

> *A week volunteering with a charity of our choice.*

What do you think of those ideas? Use the following phrases to express your own opinion on each one. Record yourself.

- I think that…
- For me…
- To be honest…
- In my opinion…
- I really feel that…
- I'm sure that…
- I guess…

**TOP TIP** Remember that a conversation is a discussion between two or more people. When you are speaking to someone don't forget to ask them questions, like 'What do you think?', 'What's your opinion?'

## AGREEING AND DISAGREEING

When having a discussion you may agree or disagree with the other person's ideas.

**(1)** Look at the following phrases. Do they express agreement or disagreement?

- I'm afraid I have to disagree
- I completely agree
- I totally disagree
- You're absolutely right
- I agree
- I'm sorry but I don't agree

In two of these phrases, the speaker starts with words to make their opinion sound more polite. Underline these words.

**TOP TIP** Remember that it is also important to explain why you agree or disagree with someone else's opinion

**(2)** Listen to the following opinions. Do you agree or disagree and why? Prepare your answers and then say them out loud.

- Living in the city is better than living in the countryside.
- The book is always better than the film.
- Sportsmen and women earn too much money.

## LINKING IDEAS AND OPINIONS

Using words and phrases to link your ideas will also make you more fluent and help the listener follow what you are saying.

The audio files for this section can be found at collins.co.uk/internationalresources.

**1** Match the following connecting phrases on the right to their correct purpose on the left.

| | | | |
|---|---|---|---|
| **A** | Starting a topic | **1** | for this reason / therefore / so / consequently |
| **B** | Ordering/sequencing | **2** | in addition to that / furthermore |
| **C** | Referring to a previous point | **3** | in summary / overall |
| **D** | Giving an example | **4** | first of all I'd like to say that |
| **E** | Adding to a point | **5** | firstly / then / next / after that |
| **F** | Expressing cause | **6** | in comparison / on the other hand / in contrast |
| **G** | Expressing result | **7** | a good example of this is |
| **H** | Comparing and contrasting | **8** | the reason why is that |
| **I** | Summarising | **9** | as I said before |

> **TOP TIP** You do not have to use all of these expressions so you could choose a few that are easy to remember. It is, however, helpful to understand the other phrases so that you can follow what other people are saying more easily.

**2** Prepare to give a short talk in which you express your opinions and use the above expressions to help people follow what you are saying. Choose one of the following topics:

**a)** The best and worst places to visit in my country.

**b)** The good and bad things about my school.

**c)** Celebrities – a good or bad influence on young people?

To prepare for your talk, start by brainstorming what you already know. For example:

- Vocabulary: how many words related to this topic can you write down in two minutes?
- What do you know about the topic?
- Has there been anything in the news recently that relates to this topic?
- Do you have any personal experience that you can use as an anecdote?

Then decide on your opinion and note the two main reasons for your argument. Consider what an opposite opinion may be and why you disagree with it. Think about what your conclusion will be.

**3** Giving a proposal: The Teenage Time Capsule

Imagine that you have been asked to come up with ideas for a teenage time capsule. The idea is to bury a box in the ground. This box should contain five items which will show future generations about life as a teenager today.

Think about which five objects you would include. What do they show about teenage life today?

Prepare and then record your proposal. Listen to the recording. Did you clearly express and give reasons for your opinions?

# ④ Developing the conversation

## USING PERSUASIVE LANGUAGE

As you develop greater fluency, you will be able to use additional skills in your conversations. Sometimes you may need to influence others, and using persuasive language will help you to achieve this.

Examples of persuasive language:
- I strongly believe
- It is my firm belief
- I can assure you
- I'm certain
- I promise
- Rest assured
- I'm sure you'll agree
- From my experience
- I definitely think
- Trust me

① Imagine that you would like to be elected for a position of responsibility at your school such as Head Boy/Girl, Sports Captain, Drama Club leader (or any idea of your own.) You need to give a speech to the whole school, explaining why you would be the best person for the role.

- Think about the points you will make and the kind of language you will use to persuade people to vote for you.
- You may want to make brief notes or bullet points of your ideas before you speak.
- You should talk for 2–3 minutes.
- Remember that if you have an audience you may be asked questions.
- When you respond, try to expand your ideas and convince the voters further!

> **TOP TIP**
> Using rhetorical questions and repetition can make your speech more powerful.
> **Rhetorical question:** a question which does not need an answer but is used to make listeners think.
> *Do you want your school to be a better place?*
> **Repetition:** repeating the same word or phrase several times for emphasis.
> *I **promise** that I'll do everything I can to improve the sports equipment, I **promise** that I'll work hard to introduce healthy options to the lunch menu, and I **promise** that I'll do my best to create a better environment for us all.*

## ADVANTAGES AND DISADVANTAGES

Discussion topics often present an opportunity to consider the advantages and disadvantages of an idea.

**1** Look at the statement below:

> *Traffic should be banned from city centres so that people can walk and cycle without the noise, dirt and pollution caused by cars and other vehicles.*

- Think about both the positive and negative sides of the argument.
- Practise expressing your views for and against the idea.

If you are working in a group, one person could summarise the overall opinion.

Remember these useful words and phrases:
- Firstly...
- However...
- Although...
- On the other hand...
- Finally...
- Overall...

**2** Here are some other topics for discussion. Practise expressing your views on each one.

a) What are the advantages and disadvantages of working from home?

b) Cosmetics and medicines should not be tested on animals.

c) Rules in school, the workplace and in society in general are not necessary. People should have the freedom to make their own decisions about how to act safely and responsibly.

d) What are the advantages and disadvantages of artificial intelligence?

Start a list of any other topics that interest you and practise discussing them with other students.

**3** You and your friends are deciding what to do at the weekend. Look at the pictures below and think about how you would discuss the advantages and disadvantages of each activity. Ideas for the first one have been started for you.

Horseriding
— Advantages:
  • good exercise
  • an outdoor activity
  • an activity with animals
— Disadvantages:
  • risk of accidents
  • expensive
  • not easily available

## CONTRIBUTING NEW IDEAS

When you are having a conversation or discussion, you may want to contribute ideas or make suggestions to expand the subject.

- Make sure your ideas link to the original topic.
- Make connections between the main subject of conversation and any new ideas.
- Stay focused on the topic.

**1** Look at the following situation. You are a school council representative and you are in a meeting with other students and school leaders. Here is the plan for the meeting.

> How to spend the extra $10 000 available in this year's budget.
> - Spend now or save for the future
> - Students' suggestions
> - Proposals from the Headteacher and Heads of Department

Look at the additional bullet points in the box below. Some of these ideas would be relevant when contributing to the budget discussion as they connect with the topic of conversation. However, some of the suggested comments do not link closely enough with the focus of the discussion.

| Relevant | Not relevant |
|---|---|
| ● The school could also ask parents for suggestions ✓ <br> ● Identify the most important improvements the school needs and the cost of each ✓ | ● Decide which charity the school should support with the money raised at the summer fair ✗ <br> ● Recycling should be encouraged more in school ✗ |

Think about ideas you could contribute to the meeting.

**2** Complete the speech bubbles around the main topic with ideas for expanding the discussion.

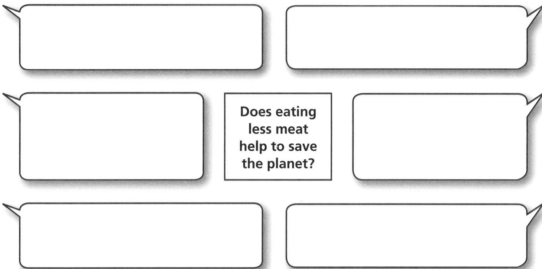

You can do this with any topic to practise developing your ideas on any given subject.

**Remember!**
- Agree or disagree with the main point of a discussion.
- Use persuasive language.
- Consider the advantages and disadvantages of the main idea.
- Contribute new ideas which are linked to the topic.
- Consider the attitudes of other countries and cultures towards the topic.
- Think beyond the present and how the topic connects with the past and the future.
- Give examples of how the topic connects with your own personal experience.

# Section 6: Synonyms

You learned about synonyms in Section 2.3. In this section, you will look at synonyms in more detail. The exercises below highlight common synonyms that relate to the topics you are studying in the Student's Book as well as some more general sets of words that you can use to talk or write about different topics. For each group of synonyms, you will first read definitions explaining the different meanings of the synonyms. Then there are exercises to practise these.

**TOP TIP** A synonym is a word or expression that has a similar meaning to another word or expression. Using synonyms can add variety to your spoken and written English. However, synonyms are rarely identical in meaning and usage. You need to learn the small differences between words, so that you can use them correctly.

## TECHNOLOGY: SYNONYMS 1

technical    technological    scientific

- **Technical** means involving machines, processes and materials used in industry, transport and communications.
- **Technological** is used to describe things which are the result of scientific knowledge being used for practical purposes, especially involving computers.
- **Scientific** is used to describe things that relate to science or to a particular science.

**1** Answer the questions, choosing from the words above.

a) Which synonym would you most likely use to describe ideas in chemistry or biology?

b) Which synonym would you most likely use to describe ideas relating to smartphones or the internet?

**2** Complete the sentences using the best adjective from the synonyms above. More than one answer may be possible.

a) Sorry, we're just having a few .............. problems. We'll get started in a minute.

b) The job requires specialist .............. knowledge.

c) In recent years, .............. advances have made video calls cheap and reliable.

d) There is new .............. research into the effects of exercise on our ability to learn.

# TECHNOLOGY: SYNONYMS 2

| device | machine | equipment | appliance | gadget |

- A **device** is an object that has been made for a particular purpose. It is often a small piece of computer equipment such as a smartphone or tablet.
- A **machine** is a piece of equipment which uses electricity or an engine in order to do a particular kind of work.
- **Equipment** consists of things such as tools or machines which are used for a particular purpose. This is a very general word and it is an uncountable noun. To talk about a single item, you can say **a piece of equipment**.
- An **appliance** is a piece of equipment such as a fridge or vacuum cleaner that does a particular job in your home.
- A **gadget** is a small piece of equipment which does a useful task. This is a less academic word we often use instead of the more formal or more specific word for something.

**3** Answer the questions, choosing from the words above.

**a)** Which TWO words are especially used to talk about something small that you can hold in your hand?

**b)** Which TWO words might be used to talk about something used in a work or industrial context?

**c)** Which word cannot be used in a plural form?

**d)** Which word would be most appropriate to refer to each of these?

   A   a smartphone or tablet

   B   a microwave

   C   something you put money in to get a ticket for a train or in a car park

   D   a small light you can attach to your smartphone for taking selfies

   E   all the things you might use to make a video, such as lights, cables etc.

**4** Match the sentence halves. Think carefully about the words in **bold**. Which words go together?

1  There's a **coffee**

2  Lots of students use **mobile**

3  The boats have all the necessary **safety**

4  Staff scan the barcode with a **handheld**

5  Research shows that using **electronic**

6  Passengers can use the **ticket**

7  It took a while to set up the **recording**

8  The apartments have new **kitchen**

A  **appliances** and air conditioning.

B  **gadgets** before bedtime can affect your sleep.

C  **machines** at the station.

D  **equipment** for the interview.

E  **device** at the entrance.

F  **equipment** on board.

G  **machine** you can use in the kitchen.

H  **devices** to watch the videos.

**TOP TIP** Look out for pairs of words that are used together: collocations. Sometimes typical collocations can help you choose the best word to use. For example, we always say coffee machine — not coffee appliance or coffee device. Write down collocations you notice in your notebook.

## TECHNOLOGY: SYNONYMS 3

| advantage | benefit | plus | positive | asset |

- An **advantage** is a way in which one thing is better than another.
- The **benefit** of something is the help that you get from it.
- A **plus** is a way in which something is good or better than something else. This is a less academic word.
- Something or someone that is an **asset** is useful or helps a person or organisation to be successful.
- A **positive** is a way in which something is good or useful.

**(5)** Answer the questions.

**a)** Which word is most used for making a comparison?

**b)** Which word would be less appropriate in an academic essay?

**c)** Which word can refer to a person who is useful to an organisation?

**d)** Complete these sentences that contain pairs of opposites.

- Each of these methods has both _____ and disadvantages.
- There are clearly _____ and minuses for each option.
- We talked about the _____ and negatives of both schemes.

**(6)** Do both the words in **bold** fit in the following sentences? If not, which word is better? Why?

**a)** The apartment's really great. It even has a view of the sea, which is a **plus/benefit**.

**b)** With all her marketing expertise, she is a great **advantage/asset** to the company.

**c)** One **advantage/benefit** of travelling by train is that it's more eco-friendly than driving.

**d)** Although we lost the game, there are some **pluses/positives** we can take from it.

**e)** As well as the physical **advantages/benefits** of regular exercise, it's good for your mental health too.

## EXPLORATION: SYNONYMS 1

| journey | trip | expedition | voyage | travels |

- If you make a **journey** somewhere, you travel there.
- A **trip** is when you travel to a place and back again. It can be a short trip to the local shops or a long trip across the world and back.
- An **expedition** is when you travel somewhere for a particular purpose such as exploration.
- A **voyage** is a long journey on a ship or in a spacecraft.
- Someone's **travels** are the journeys they make to places a long way from their home. Used in this way, this is a plural noun and refers to many journeys considered together, not just a single visit.

**1** Answer the questions, choosing from the words above.

**a)** Thinking about *journey* and *trip*, which word refers to travelling in one direction, A > B, and which word describes going somewhere and coming back, A <-> B?

**b)** Which synonym might someone use to talk about all the different places in the world they've visited?

**c)** Which synonym(s) would be most appropriate to describe travelling to Mars?

**d)** Which synonym(s) would be most appropriate to describe travelling on foot to the North Pole?

**2** Match the comments, 1–5, to the contexts, A–E.

**1** I've got lots of things in the house collected on my **travels**.

**2** The train **journey** from the airport to the city centre only took 30 minutes.

**3** I got these beautiful Russian dolls on a recent **trip** to Moscow.

**4** We set off on a three-week transatlantic **voyage**.

**5** My next scientific **expedition** will take me to some of the remotest parts of Sumatra.

**A** She regularly travels to different places.

**B** He travelled somewhere and came home again.

**C** She's travelling somewhere to carry out research.

**D** He travelled a long distance by boat.

**E** She travelled from one place to another.

## EXPLORATION: SYNONYMS 2

| understanding | knowledge | grasp | awareness |
|---|---|---|---|

- If you have an **understanding** of something, you know how it works or what it means.
- **Knowledge** is information and understanding about a subject, which someone has in their mind.
- A **grasp** of something complicated is an understanding of it.
- **Awareness** of a fact or situation is knowing about it.

**3** Answer the questions, choosing from the words above.

a) Which synonym would you use if you know that something exists, but you don't have any more information about it?

b) Which synonym would you use to talk about what you know generally about a school subject, such as history or physics?

c) Which synonym(s) would you use to talk about what you know about a specific idea, such as how gravity works or why the moon changes shape?

**4** Choose the best synonym to complete the sentences. Think about meaning and also look at the words around the gap. More than one answer may be possible.

a) The job requires specialist .............. of commercial accounting procedures.

b) We want to raise .............. of youth homelessness in the city.

c) You need to have a clear .............. of what the project involves before you start.

d) It's difficult to communicate with such a limited .............. of the language.

e) After watching the video, I had a better .............. of the application process.

f) She can draw on her medical .............. and experience when making decisions.

## HEALTH: SYNONYMS 1

| illness | disease | condition | infection | virus |
|---|---|---|---|---|

- An **illness** is a particular medical problem. It can be a minor problem such as a cold or a more serious problem such as pneumonia.
- A **disease** is a medical problem which affects people, animals or plants. It is mostly used to refer to more serious problems.
- A **condition** is a medical problem that usually lasts for a long time, such as diabetes or asthma.
- An **infection** is a disease caused by germs (= tiny living things).
- A **virus** is a kind of germ that can cause disease. We also often use the word **virus** to refer to the disease it causes. The correct word for a disease caused by a virus is a viral infection.

**1** Which synonyms would be best to describe each of these medical problems. More than one answer may be possible.

a) diabetes

b) a cold

c) Covid-19

d) a sore throat

e) cancer

f) mildew (a problem that affects plants)

**2** Do both the words in **bold** fit in the following sentences? If not, which word is better? Why?

a) The clinic deals with the patients with minor **illnesses/diseases** or injuries.

b) He suffers from a **disease/condition** called sleep apnea which affects his breathing at night.

c) This **illness/disease** has caused the death of thousands of frogs worldwide.

d) The flu **infection/virus** is spread mainly by touching surfaces and then touching your face.

e) Regular exercise can lower your risk of heart **disease/illness**.

f) The singer had to cancel the gig because of a throat **disease/infection**.

## HEALTH: SYNONYMS 2

| problem | difficulty | trouble | challenge |
|---|---|---|---|

- A **problem** is an unsatisfactory situation that causes difficulties for people.
- A **difficulty** is a problem. If you are **in difficulty**, you are having a lot of problems. If you **have difficulty** doing something, you are not able to do it easily.
- You can refer to problems as **trouble**. If you say that one aspect of a situation is **the trouble**, you mean that it is the aspect which is causing problems.
- A **challenge** is something new and difficult which requires great effort and determination. We sometimes use challenge in a more positive way to say that something is difficult but we can manage to deal with it.

**3** Answer the questions, choosing from the words above.

- Which word(s) would you use to describe a specific situation such as forgetting your password for a website or not having enough chairs for everyone to sit on?
- Which word(s) would you use to describe a situation which was not easy for many reasons, such as trying to find a job or communicating in a country where you don't speak the language?
- Which word(s) would you use in a job interview to describe a situation in which you had to deal with new things?

**(4)** Choose the best synonym to complete the sentences. Think about meaning and how the word fits grammatically. More than one answer may be possible.

**a)** Sorry we're late. We had .............. finding a parking space.

**b)** Stress can cause serious health ................

**c)** I could see the swimmer was in .............., so I called the lifeguard.

**d)** He suffers from knee pain and he sometimes has .............. getting upstairs.

**e)** My biggest .............. was overcoming my nerves when I speak in front of people.

**f)** The .............. with this approach is that it doesn't suit everyone.

**g)** Wheelchair users face two main .............. on campus: steps and narrow doorways.

**h)** The new government's first .............. is the economy.

> **TOP TIP**
>
> Pay attention to the grammar of words and how they are used in a sentence as well as the meaning. For example, we often use *problem* to talk about specific issues; *a problem, two problems, several problems*. We can use *difficulty* and *trouble* (as uncountable nouns) to talk more generally about the fact that a situation is not easy; *have trouble/difficulty doing something*. Or we can talk about *the difficulty or the trouble* (the + singular noun) to refer to the main issue in a situation.

### HEALTH: SYNONYMS 3

| prevent | avoid | stop |
|---------|-------|------|

- If you **prevent** something, you stop it happening, especially by taking action in advance.
- If you **avoid** something unpleasant that might happen, you take action or change your plans in order to stop it from happening.
- If you **stop** something, you prevent it from happening or continuing.

**(5)** Answer the questions, choosing from the words above.

**a)** Which synonym can you use when something unpleasant still happens, but you change your plans so it doesn't affect you?

**b)** Which synonym can you use when something starts, but you do something so it doesn't continue?

**(6)** Complete the descriptions using the most appropriate synonym. More than one answer may be possible.

**a)** We were out walking when it suddenly started raining, so we stood under some trees to .............. getting wet.

**b)** Eating healthily and taking regular exercise can help to .............. heart disease and other serious illnesses.

**c)** In hot weather, make sure you drink plenty of water to .............. becoming dehydrated.

**d)** Several boys were playing football on the grass, until the police arrived and .............. the game.

**e)** Warming up properly before you exercise is important to .............. injuries.

**f)** Maya is partially sighted, but that doesn't .............. her from doing many of the same activities as her friends.

## EDUCATION: SYNONYMS 1

| learn | master | pick up |

- When you **learn**, you obtain knowledge or a skill through studying or training.
- If you **master** something, you manage to learn how to do it properly or understand it completely.
- If you **pick up** a skill or an idea, you acquire it without effort. This is a less academic word.

**(1)** Answer the questions, choosing from the words above.

**a)** Which word would you use to describe something you learn without trying?

**b)** Which word(s) would you use to talk about something you understand fully now?

**(2)** Match the sentence halves. More than one answer may be possible.

**1** I **picked up** a few words of Spanish

**2** I'm **learning** Spanish

**3** I **learned** to swim

**4** I've **mastered** the basic dance steps

**5** I **picked up** some cookery skills

**6** I finally **mastered** a skateboard trick

**A** at school.

**B** by playing with the local kids when we were on holiday.

**C** that I've been practising for weeks.

**D** and now I'm ready to put them together into a routine.

**E** from helping my mum in the kitchen

**F** when I was a young kid.

## EDUCATION: SYNONYMS 2

| affect | influence | impact |

- When something **affects** someone or something, it has an effect on them.
- If someone or something **influences** people or events, they affect the way people think or act, or what happens.
- If something **impacts** a situation or person or **impacts on** them, it has a strong effect on them. We typically use impact to describe a strong negative effect (negatively/severely/adversely impact). You can use it to talk about a strong positive effect, but you need to say 'positively impact'.

**(3)** Answer the questions, choosing from the words above.

**a)** Which synonym describes something causing a significant change?

**b)** Which synonym describes how something may be just one part of what causes a change?

**c)** Which synonym is mostly used to talk about negative effects?

**d)** Which TWO synonyms can also be used as nouns? Which word has a different noun form?

**(4)** Choose the best word in **bold** to complete the sentences.

● More than seven million people have been **affected/influenced** by floods.

● We need to understand the ways in which social media is **affecting/impacting** on young people's lives.

● What you eat may **influence/impact** your risk of getting certain diseases.

● Some students said not having a quiet place to study negatively **influenced/impacted** their schoolwork.

● The timetable changes only **affect/influence** morning classes.

● Both your friends and your parents **influence/affect** the decisions you make about what subjects to study.

## COMPETITION: SYNONYMS 1

| approve of | agree with | support |
|---|---|---|

● If you **approve of** something or someone, you like them or think they are good.

● If you **agree with** an action or a suggestion, you think it is a good thing.

● If you **support** someone or their ideas, you like them and want them to succeed.

**(1)** Complete the sentences with a preposition (*of, with*) in each gap. If no preposition is needed, write –.

**a)** Some people don't **agree** ............... eating meat.

**b)** 75% of people **approve** ............... the plans to encourage more electric cars.

**c)** We fully **support** ............... the teacher's decision to ban mobiles in class.

**d)** I don't **approve** ............... dividing students into groups according to ability.

**e)** She strongly **supported** ............... the campaign to reduce the speed limit in the city centre.

**f)** Most people **agreed** ............... the decision to allow students to bring mobile phones into the classroom.

**(2)** Which of the ideas above do you agree with? Use different synonyms to express your opinion. Add expressions like *completely, definitely, fully, strongly, not really.*

Pay attention to the prepositions (*of, with*, etc.) used with different words and expressions. Write them in your vocabulary notebook together.
Be careful, sometimes words have a different meaning with and without a preposition:
*The manager approved of the plans.* = she liked them
*The manager approved the plans.* = she gave official permission for them to go ahead.

## COMPETITION: SYNONYMS 2

| reason | cause | purpose | motive | grounds |
|--------|-------|---------|--------|---------|

- The **reason** for something is a fact or situation which explains why it happens.
- The **cause** of an event is the thing that makes it happen.
- The **purpose** of something is the reason for which it is made or done.
- Your **motive** for doing something is your reason for doing it. Someone's motive is the thoughts or feelings that explain their behaviour.
- The **grounds** for doing something are the reason or justification for it. This is a more formal word. It is usually plural.

**3** Which of the synonyms above would be best to describe each context? More than one word may be possible. Explain your choice(s).

a) The train was delayed because a tree had fallen down and blocked the line.

b) We installed a ramp to help wheelchair users access the building.

c) I bought the t-shirt because I really liked the colour.

d) I took my sister out for lunch because I wanted to ask her a favour.

e) I don't buy water in plastic bottles because I'm concerned about plastic waste.

**4** Complete the sentences using one of the synonyms above. Think about meaning and the words around the gap.

a) Police are investigating the ............... of the accident.

b) The main ............... of her visit was to see her elderly grandmother.

c) We still don't understand the ............... for the attack. Why would someone do something like that?

d) The first option was ruled out on the ............... of cost.

e) My main ............... for moving to the city was to find work.

f) The most common ............... of injuries among runners is not warming up properly.

g) There may be a good ............... why she left early.

h) The mats serve a practical ............... – protecting the table, as well as looking pretty.

## WORK: SYNONYMS 1

| job | career | occupation | profession | employment |

- A **job** is the work that someone does to earn money.
- Your **career** is your job, a series of jobs or the part of your life that you spend working.
- Your **occupation** is your job or the type of work you do. This is a slightly formal word that is used especially on forms or to describe types of work.
- A **profession** is a type of job that requires advanced education or training.
- If you are in **employment**, you have a paid job. This is an uncountable noun used to talk generally about the fact of having work.

**(1)** Answer the questions, choosing from the words above.

- Which of the synonym(s) would you use to talk about the work you do now for a specific employer?
- Which of the synonyms could you use to talk about the work you've done over time for more than one employer?
- Which of the synonyms could you use to talk about the work you normally do even if you are not working at the moment?

**(2)** Choose the best synonym to complete each sentence. More than one answer may be possible.

a) During her long ................, she worked at museums in Paris, New York and Amsterdam.

b) The survey includes questions about your age, religion, education and ................ .

c) I've applied for several ................, but I haven't had any interviews yet.

d) 56% of university graduates went straight into full-time ................ .

e) She has a part-time ................ working in a local bookshop.

f) Working in the medical ................ often involves long hours.

## WORK: SYNONYMS 2

| manage | run | be in charge of |

- If someone **manages** an organisation, business, or system, they are responsible for controlling it. A **manager** is often in control of other workers and making decisions.
- If you **run** an organisation or an activity, you are responsible for it or you organise it. If you **run** something, you are involved in all the tasks of the business. You can run a small business without any employees.
- If you **are in charge of** something or someone, you have responsibility for them.

**3** Answer the questions, choosing from the words above.

- Which synonym(s) can you use to talk about being responsible for other people?
- Which synonym(s) could you use to describe someone who has their own small shop?
- Which synonym(s) could you use to talk about someone who has responsibility for a particular task as part of a team?

**4** Match the people to the statements.

1 Amy makes jewellery which she sells on a market stall.

2 Marisa is the head of an IT department with six staff.

3 The tennis coach asked Ravi to make sure the nets are in place before each training session.

4 Nelson is the person responsible for redesigning the new office.

5 Agnes set up a charity which provides meals to older people in the village.

6 Pascal is responsible for online marketing

A She **manages** the team.

B He's **in charge of** setting the equipment up.

C She **runs** the service.

D He's **managing** the project.

E She **runs** a small business.

F He's **in charge of** that part of the business.

## WORK: SYNONYMS 3

| disadvantage | drawback | downside | trouble |

- A **disadvantage** is a part of a situation which causes problems. We often compare advantages and disadvantages.
- A **drawback** is an aspect of something that makes it less acceptable.
- **The downside** of a situation is the aspect of it which is less positive, pleasant or useful than its other aspects. This is usually a singular noun.
- If you say that one aspect of a situation is **the trouble,** you mean that it is the aspect which is causing problems. This is always a single noun and it is a less academic word.

**5** Answer the questions, choosing from the words above.

a) Which two synonyms can be plural and which two are usually singular?

b) Which word would be less suitable in a formal academic essay?

c) Which word(s) could you use to compare the good points and bad points of something?

**6** Match the sentence halves. Think about both meaning and grammar.

| | |
|---|---|
| **1** Being based in Bangkok has both advantages | **A** include less privacy and more noise. |
| **2** The biggest **drawback** with this approach | **B** outweigh the benefits. |
| **3** The only **downside** of the job | **C** is the light reflects on my laptop screen. |
| **4** Some of the **drawbacks** of an open-plan office | **D** is the early-morning starts. |
| **5** The **trouble** with having my desk by the window | **E** is the high cost. |
| **6** I think the **disadvantages** of working from home | **F** and **disadvantages**. |

## ENVIRONMENT AND WILDLIFE: SYNONYMS 1

| damage | harm | destroy | ruin |
|---|---|---|---|

- If you **damage** something, you injure or harm it.
- If you **harm** someone or something you injure or damage them.
- To **destroy** something means to cause so much damage to it that it is completely ruined or does not exist any more.
- To **ruin** something means to severely harm, damage or spoil it.

**1** Answer the questions.

**a)** Which two synonyms describe the most severe negative effect?

**b)** Which verb(s) can describe a negative effect on a person?

**c)** Which of the verbs have the same noun forms? Which one is different?

**2** Choose the best verb to describe these situations.

**a)** Farmers cut down all the trees to grow crops. They ............... the forest.

**b)** I dropped my phone and now it has a small scratch on the screen. I ............... it.

**c)** The protest was completely peaceful with no violence. The protestors didn't ............... anyone.

**d)** This area of countryside used to be beautiful and peaceful before they built a motorway through it. It's completely ............... it.

**e)** Plastic waste can be eaten by animals or get caught around them and cause injuries. It can ............... wildlife.

**f)** The scandal was really bad for the company. It badly ............... their reputation.

## ENVIRONMENT AND WILDLIFE: SYNONYMS 2

| responsible for | to blame for | at fault | guilty of |
|---|---|---|---|

- If someone or something is **are responsible for** something bad that has happened, they are the cause of it.
- If someone or something **is to blame for** something bad that has happened, they caused it. This phrase is especially used to express an opinion.
- If someone or something is **at fault**, they caused a particular situation that has gone wrong.
- If someone **is guilty of** doing something wrong or committing a crime, they have done that thing or committed a crime.

**3** Answer the questions choosing from the phrases above.

**a)** Which phrase(s) would you most likely use to describe a specific action that caused a problem?

**b)** Which phrase(s) would be most appropriate to describe a legal case?

**c)** Which phrases can you use when:

A  the cause of a problem is a person

B  the cause of a problem is a thing

**4** Complete the sentences using the word in brackets. Add any other words that are needed. The first one has been done for you.

**a)** (responsible) The company is investigating who was .responsible for. the error.

**b)** (fault) Both the driver and the cyclist are ............... the accident. The driver was going too fast, but the cyclist pulled out without looking.

**c)** (blame) I think supermarkets are at least partly ............... the amount of plastic packaging on food.

**d)** (guilty) I believe the company is ............... discrimination in this case.

**e)** (responsible) Back pain is ............... more lost working days than any other illness.

**f)** (blame) It's difficult to know who's ............... this whole mess.

| amount | number | quantity |
|--------|--------|----------|

- **An amount of** something is how much of it you have, need or get. You use **amount of** with uncountable nouns such as *time*, *money* and *information*.

- You use **number** with adjectives such as *large* or *small* to say approximately how many things or people there are. If there are **a number of** things or people, there are several of them. You use **number of** with countable nouns such as *people*, *things* and *problems*.

- A **quantity** is an amount that you can measure or count. We often use quantity with adjectives such as *large* or *small*. You can use quantity with countable and uncountable nouns. It is a slightly more formal word mostly used in writing.

**(5)** Answer the questions, choosing from the words above.

**a)** Which synonyms can you use to say how many *books* or *cars* or *trees* there are?

**b)** Which synonyms can you use to say how much *water* or *food* there is?

**c)** Can *amount* and *number* always be replaced by *quantity*?

**(6)** Complete the sentences using one of the synonyms above and the best form of a noun from the box. Different answers may be possible.

| consumer | damage | food | information | ticket | time | tourist | vitamin |
|----------|--------|------|-------------|--------|------|---------|---------|

**a)** It's New Zealand's largest lake and attracts a large ..number of tourists.. in the summer.

**b)** The wild fire caused a huge .............. to the wildlife in the area.

**c)** Book quickly as there are only a limited ............ available for this event!

**d)** The scheme aims to reduce the ............ wasted by households.

**e)** Parents worry about the ............ their children spend staring at screens.

**f)** All foods contain small .............. .

**g)** We see an increasing .............. who check prices online before they come into the store.

**h)** Social networking sites collect vast .............. about their users.

> **TOP TIP**
> You can say either **a large number/amount/quantity of** something or **large numbers/amounts/quantities of** something. If you are talking about a specific quantity in a particular place at a particular time, you use the singular form: *I only added a small amount of salt.* If you are talking more generally, you can use the singular or plural form: *Eating large amounts/a large amount of salt can be bad for your health.*

## CULTURE AND SOCIETY: SYNONYMS 1

| traditional | old-fashioned | established | conventional |

- **Traditional** customs, beliefs and methods are ones that have existed for a long time.
- Something that is **old-fashioned** is no longer used, done or believed by most people, because it has been replaced by something that is more modern.
- An **established** person or organisation has a good reputation, usually because they have existed for a long time.
- A **conventional** method or product is the one that is usually used. We often use conventional to contrast with something new and different.

**1** Answer the questions, choosing from the synonyms above.

- Which of the synonyms have a positive or a negative feeling? Which ones are more neutral?
- Which word is mostly used to describe people or groups of people?
- Which of these two cars could you describe as *old-fashioned* and which one is *conventional*? Why might you use the word *conventional* here?

**2** Match the sentences to the comments that follow on.

1. Most of the writers speaking at the book festival are **established** names.

2. The school doesn't use **conventional** teaching methods.

3. Paella is a **traditional** Spanish dish based on rice.

4. The company has a very **old-fashioned** way of working.

5. The chairs are handmade using **traditional** techniques.

A. People have been making it here for generations.

B. They're not mass-produced in a factory, then.

C. They really need to modernise their processes.

D. So, I'll probably know them already, then.

E. So, what are they doing that's so new and different?

## CULTURE AND SOCIETY: SYNONYMS 2

| modern | contemporary | current | up-to-date |
|---|---|---|---|

- **Modern** means relating to the present time. Something that is **modern** is new and involves the latest ideas or equipment.
- **Contemporary** means existing now or at the time you are talking about.
- Something that is **current** is happening, being done or being used now.
- If something is **up-to-date**, it is the newest thing of its kind. This can be spelled as **up-to-date**, especially before a noun or **up to date**, especially after a verb.

**3** Answer the questions, choosing from the words above.

- Which synonym can describe something now or at a particular time in the past?
- Which words can be used to talk about the general time around now, for example, in the last ten years?
- Which words describe something really new?

**4** Match the sentence halves. Think carefully about the words in **bold**. Which words go together?

| | |
|---|---|
| 1 The hotel has a simple **contemporary** | A **life** like constant mobile phone alerts. |
| 2 You can find **up-to-date** | B **system** is not working as it should. |
| 3 It's thanks to **modern** | C **accounts** of the French Revolution. |
| 4 In history, we read some **contemporary** | D **information** about opening times on our website. |
| 5 It's hard to escape the distractions of **modern** | E **design** and excellent facilities. |
| 6 It's clear that the **current** | F **medicine** that people are living active lives into their 80s. |

## TRANSPORT: SYNONYMS 1

| fast | quick | rapid | express |
|---|---|---|---|

- **Fast** means moving, acting or happening with great speed.
- Someone or something that is **quick** moves or does things with great speed.
- If something is **rapid**, it happens or moves very quickly. This word is slightly formal and less used in everyday conversation.
- An **express** service is one in which things are done faster than usual. An **express** train or bus is faster than usual and stops at fewer places. This adjective is always used before a noun.

**1** Answer the questions, choosing from the words above.

a) Which adjective would be most appropriate to describe movement of the highest speed; quick or fast?

b) Which TWO adjectives would be best to describe something that changes or develops in a short time?

c) Which adjective describes a limited range of things?

**2** Choose the best adjective to describe each context. More than one answer may be possible.

a) A car that can drive at high speeds. A(n) .............. car.

b) A train that makes a journey between two places in a short time. A(n) .............. train.

c) When you look at something for only a short time. A(n) .............. look.

d) When something makes a lot of progress in a short time. .............. progress.

e) A decision you make without thinking for too long. A(n) .............. decision.

f) A delivery service that arrives in a shorter time than usual. A(n) .............. delivery.

g) When something spreads a lot in a short time. The .............. spread of the fire.

h) The route between two places that will take the least time. The .............. route.

> **TOP TIP**
> You can increase your vocabulary and make your writing more interesting by learning and using other forms of a word. There are often adverb forms of adjectives; *quick – quickly, rapid – rapidly. the rapid spread of the fire / the fire spread rapidly.* But remember *fast* has the same form as an adjective and an adverb: *a fast runner / she ran fast.*

## TRANSPORT: SYNONYMS 2

| develop | grow | progress | advance |
|---------|------|----------|---------|

- When someone or something **develops**, or when someone **develops** something, the person or thing grows or changes over a period of time and usually becomes more advanced or complete.
- When something or someone **grows**, they develop and increase in size or intensity.
- To **progress** means to improve or to become stronger or more advanced.
- To **advance** means to make progress in something, especially in your knowledge of something.

**3** Answer the questions, choosing from the words above.

a) Which verb(s) would you use to describe a plant or animal getting bigger in size?

b) All the verbs can be used as intransitive verbs; to say something develops /grows / progresses /advances. Which verb(s) can also be used as transitive verbs to say that someone .............. s something?

**4** Match the sentence halves.

| | |
|---|---|
| 1 Medical technology has | A **advanced** considerably. |
| 2 She has written about how children | B **progressing** as quickly as he expected. |
| 3 There's a risk that the disease can | C **grew** by 3.5 million. |
| 4 The country's population | D greener technologies. |
| 5 The company is **developing** | E **develop**, grow and learn. |
| 6 He felt he wasn't | F **progress** rapidly. |

## FASHION: SYNONYMS 1

| clothes | clothing | dress | outfit |
|---|---|---|---|

- **Clothes** are the things that people wear, such as shirts, coats, trousers and dresses. It is always a plural noun.
- **Clothing** is the clothes people wear. This is a slightly more formal word. It is an uncountable noun used to talk about clothes in general or a particular type of clothes, e.g. *protective clothing*. You can talk about **an item of clothing** to refer to a particular shirt or jacket, etc.
- You can refer to clothes worn by men or women as **dress**. This is an uncountable noun often used in phrases such as *style of dress, casual/traditional dress*.
- An **outfit** is a set of clothes or all the clothes someone is wearing together.

**1** Answer the questions, choosing from the words above.

a) Which of the synonyms would you use in everyday conversation to talk about what someone is wearing?

b) What's the difference between *dress* (uncountable) and *a dress* (countable)?

c) What's the difference between *clothes* and *cloth*?

**2** Choose the best word in **bold** to complete the sentences.

a) I love your **outfit / dress**; that top goes really well with those trousers.

b) You can take up to four items of **clothes / clothing** into the changing room.

c) The men wore traditional Pakistani **dress / dresses**.

d) Make sure you bring warm **clothes / dress**; it gets chilly in the evenings.

e) The event is sponsored by a well-known **clothes / clothing** brand.

f) I need to buy some new **cloths / clothes** for my summer holiday.

## FASHION: SYNONYMS 2

| process | procedure | system | method |
|---------|-----------|--------|--------|

- A **process** is a series of actions or events which have a particular result.
- A **procedure** is a way of doing something, especially the usual or correct way.
- A **system** is a way of working, organising, or doing something which follows a fixed plan or set of rules.
- A **method** is a particular way of doing something.

**(3)** Answer the questions, choosing from the words above.

**a)** Which synonym emphasises the particular way that something is done?

**b)** Which synonyms describe the steps involved in doing something?

**c)** Which synonym has the most general meaning, which can include the steps needed to do something, the way it is done and all the things that go around it?

**(4)** Choose the best synonym to talk about each context.

**a)** First, you fill in an online application form, then you might be asked to complete a more detailed questionnaire. Finally, you're invited for an interview. That's the application ............... .

**b)** The form must be checked and signed by your manager. That's the correct ............... .

**c)** The costumes are all sewn by hand from local silk. They're made using traditional ............... .

**d)** In case of a fire, everyone must leave the building immediately using the stairs. That's the safety ............... .

**e)** Kindergartens, primary and secondary schools, colleges and universities are all part of the education ............... .

**f)** The olives are picked and transported to the factory where they're washed, crushed to a paste and finally pressed to extract the oil. The whole production ............... takes less than 24 hours.

## ENTERTAINMENT: SYNONYMS 1

| programme | show | series | season | episode |
|-----------|------|--------|--------|---------|

- A television or radio **programme** is something that is broadcast on television or radio.
- A television or radio **show** is a programme on television or radio.
- A radio or television **series** is a set of related programmes with the same title.
- A set of television programmes with the same title and broadcast at the same time is known as a **season**, e.g. season 1, season 2, etc. This is an American English word that is becoming more common in British English.
- An **episode** is one of the programmes in a series on television or radio.

**1** Answer the questions, choosing from the words above.

**a)** Which words can refer to a single broadcast on radio or TV?

**b)** Which TWO words refer to a number of related broadcasts? Are they exact synonyms?

**c)** Which word often has another word before it describing the type of broadcast, e.g. chat/quiz/game/reality/talent .................?

**2** Match the sentence halves.

| | |
|---|---|
| **1** The final **episode** | **A** will be shown next Sunday. |
| **2** The second **season** of | **B** is set in the Kenyan capital, Nairobi. |
| **3** She's the presenter of a popular | **C** children's TV **programme**. |
| **4** This new six-part drama **series** | **D** **show** as a singer in a teenage girl band. |
| **5** She first appeared on a TV talent | **E** the hit comedy starts next week. |

## ENTERTAINMENT: SYNONYMS 2

| for | in favour of | pro |
|---|---|---|

- If you are **for** something, you think it is a good thing.
- If you are **in favour of** something, you think that it is a good thing.
- If you are **pro** something, you agree with it or support it. The prefix **pro-** also forms adjectives that refer to people who strongly support a particular person or thing, e.g. *pro-democracy*.

**3** Answer the questions, choosing from the words above.

**a)** Which synonym is often joined to another word to describe the thing which someone supports?

**b)** Complete the pairs of opposites:

**A** People can be ............... or against something.

**B** People can be ............... something or opposed to it.

**C** People can be ............... or anti an idea or belief.

**4** Complete the paragraphs from two essays using a mix of the synonyms above.

When people are asked whether they are [1]............... or against reducing traffic, most people will say they are [2]............... having fewer cars on the roads. However, although most of us are [3]............... the idea of quieter roads in theory, we don't actually want to give up our own cars.

Unsurprisingly, 4 ................. –government news channels have been largely positive about the decision to build a new airport. They print quotes from people who are 5 ................. the development and emphasise the arguments 6 ................. expanding air travel.

## ENTERTAINMENT: SYNONYMS 3

| against | opposed to | anti |
|---------|-----------|------|

- If you are **against** an idea, policy or system, you think it is wrong.
- If you are **opposed to** something, you disagree with it or disapprove of it.
- If someone is opposed to something, you can say that they are **anti** it. **Anti-** is used to form adjectives and nouns that describe someone or something that is opposed to a particular system, practice, or group of people, e.g. *anti-government*.

**5** Match the descriptions to the people.

1 Both women strongly believe that people should not be discriminated against.

2 The organisers hope the protests will be peaceful.

3 Most ordinary cricket fans don't want the rules to change.

4 Students are very unhappy about plans to charge more for university courses.

5 Many local people disagree with new houses being built by the river.

6 The couple are vegetarians, but they don't think everyone should be.

A They're strongly **opposed to** the plans.

B They're not **anti** meat-eating.

C They're **against** the changes.

D They're bitterly **opposed to** increasing fees.

E They're **anti**-racism campaigners.

F They're totally **against** violence.

## YOUNG AND OLD: SYNONYMS 1

| young person | youth | teenager | teen | adolescent |
|--------------|-------|----------|------|------------|

- You can refer to people in the early years of their life, especially between the ages of around thirteen to twenty-five, as **young people**.
- Journalists sometimes refer to mostly young men as **youths**. The word is usually used in a negative context, especially where the young men have caused trouble.
- A **teenager** is someone between thirteen and nineteen years of age.
- A **teen** is someone between thirteen and nineteen years of age. This is a more informal word.
- An **adolescent** is a young person who is no longer a child but who has not yet become an adult. This word is especially used when talking about the stages of a person's development.

**1)** Answer the questions, choosing from the words above.

a) Which synonym has a negative sense?

b) Which synonym is more informal?

c) Which synonym would you most likely find in a medical text?

d) Which synonym(s) could you use to describe someone in their early 20s?

**2)** Choose the best word in bold to complete the sentences.

a) Residents complained about noise from a group of **adolescents/youths** in the nearby park.

b) According to research, school-age children and **teens/teenagers** should get at least nine hours of sleep a day.

c) The campaign aims to address mental health problems among **young people/youths**.

d) The film follows a group of bored **adolescents/teens** over the course of a wild weekend.

e) Active **adolescents/young people** need healthy carbohydrates to provide the glucose that their brains need.

f) The average **youth/young person** gets between four and seven hours of screen time per day.

## YOUNG AND OLD: SYNONYMS 2

| old | older | middle-aged | elderly | ageing |
|-----|-------|-------------|---------|--------|

- Someone who is **old** has lived for many years and is no longer young. Describing someone as old can have negative connotations and in many contexts is not polite.
- You can use **older** as a more polite way of talking about someone who is not young. An older person could be in any age group from about 40 upwards.
- **Middle-aged** people are between the ages of about 40 and 60.
- You use **elderly** as a polite way of saying that someone is old. An elderly person is usually past working age.
- Someone who is **ageing** is becoming older and less healthy.

**3)** Answer the questions, choosing from the words above.

a) Which synonym(s) can be less polite?

b) Which word(s) could be used to describe someone in their 50s?

c) Which word(s) could be used to describe someone in their 80s?

**4** Match the sentence halves.

**1** If you ask children to draw a scientist, they tend to draw an **old**

**2** On days of higher air pollution, more **older**

**3** Many countries with an **ageing**

**4** We got chatting to a couple of **older**

**5** Sitting opposite me were a **middle-aged**

**6** She helped out her **elderly**

**A** population face increasing healthcare costs.

**B** man who looks like Einstein.

**C** couple with their teenage daughter.

**D** women who were visiting for the day.

**E** neighbours by doing shopping for them.

**F** people need hospital treatment for lung problems.

## YOUNG AND OLD: SYNONYMS 3

| person | individual | human | population | the public |

- A **person** is a man, woman or child. The normal plural form is **people**. Persons is only used in very formal, official and legal contexts.
- An **individual** is a person, especially when considered on their own rather than as part of a group.
- You can refer to people as **humans** or **human beings** when you are comparing them with animals or machines.
- The **population** of a place is the people who live there, or the number of people living there.
- You can refer to people in general as **the public** or **the general public**, especially when comparing them to a special group such as politicians, the police, celebrities or scientists. The public can be followed by either a singular or a plural verb; the public is/are. You can use a member of the public to talk about one person.

**5** Answer the questions, choosing from the words above.

**a)** Which synonym(s) can be used to talk about a single man or woman?

**b)** Which synonym(s) are always used to talk about a group of people?

**c)** Which word is especially used when talking people in contrast to:

**A** computers

**B** specialists

**6** Complete the sentences using one of the synonyms above. More than one answer may be possible.

a) Tickets go on sale to the general .................. on 1st July.

b) It is impossible to identify the .................. in the video footage.

c) Swimmer Michael Phelps was the first .................. to win eight gold medals in one Olympic Games.

d) The city's .................. has almost doubled in ten years.

e) The disease is thought to have moved from animals to ...................

f) 61 per cent of the adult .................. has a credit card.

g) The email does not name any .................. accused of bullying.

h) The alarm was raised by a member of .................. who saw smoke coming from the building.

> **TOP TIP**
>
> You can make your writing more interesting by using more specific words to refer to different types or groups of people; consumers, shoppers, workers, local residents, internet users, motorists, parents, passengers, etc.

# Acknowledgements

The publishers gratefully acknowledge the permission granted to reproduce the copyright material in this book. While every effort has been made to trace and contact copyright holders, where this has not been possible the publishers will be pleased to make the necessary arrangements at the first opportunity.

Extract on p.6 from Basketball Camp Spain; Extracts on pp. 12–13 from 'Riders prepare for Mongol Derby: toughest horserace in the world' by Amy Mathieson, *Horse and Hound* magazine, 18/06/2009, copyright © Horse & Hound/IPC+ Syndication; Extract on p.75 from 'Anxiety and fear in children' copyright © 2017 State of Victoria. This information has been provided by the Better Health Channel.

The publisher would like to thank the following for permission to reproduce pictures in these pages (t = top, b = bottom, c = centre, l = left, r = right):

p6 ESB Professional/Shutterstock, pp12 and 13 andrewwheeler.com/ Alamy Stock Photo, p12b Andrew Krasnik/Shutterstock, p17tr Daxiao Productions/Shutterstock, p22 Narupom Nimpaiboom/Shutterstock, p27 solarseven/Shutterstock, p44 SIHASAKPRACHUM/Shutterstock, p44 Khafizov Ivan Harisovich/Shutterstock, p50 Photononstop/Alamy, p71 Krasula/Shutterstock, p72 Studio MARMILADE/ Shutterstock, p86 Skylines/Shutterstock, p86 Daniel Lamborn/Shutterstock, p86 Vasin Lee/Shutterstock, p96tr santypan/Shutterstock, p97 John Kershner/ Shutterstock, p101 Syda Productions/Shutterstock, p102 buzzbee/ Shutterstock, p106 AmySachar/Shutterstock, p107 Em7/Shutterstock, p109 William Perugini/ Shutterstock, p111br alfocome/Shutterstock, p112 michaeljung/Shutterstock, p113 NadyGinzburg/Shutterstock, p114tl Fotokostic/Shutterstock, p114tr Juan Miguel Cervera Merlo/ Shutterstock, p114cl Monkey Business Images/ Shutterstock, p114cr Prostock-studio/Shutterstock, p114b Odua Images/Shutterstock, p124br Firn/Shutterstock, p131l Monkey Business Images/ Shutterstock , p131r Martin Charles Hatch/ Shutterstock.